Sunset

Memories of
My Mother

Sunset

*Memories of
My Mother*

BY

Steven Michael Hubele

Sunset
Memories of My Mother

ISBN: 978-0-9885877-2-4

Published by Stephen Michael Hubele
314-631-6779 • stevehubele@charter.net
St. Louis, MO

Book design by Peggy Nehmen, n-kcreative.com

Printed in the United States of America

To Aunt Rose, Sister Leonette,
my three sisters, and all the dedicated
professionals who work with sick and dying
elderly patients on a daily basis.

In memory of my mother.

Also by Stephen Michael Hubele:

Almost Full Circle: A Tribute to Dad
The Hobsons of Rainbow Creek: A Tea Party Novel

Acknowledgements

I have a lot of people to thank for this book. First and foremost are my mother, Audrey (Juengst) Hubele, and my aunt, Rosemarie (Juengst) Holley-Mock. Their encouragement helped me push through difficult hurdles along the way, in life and in my writing efforts.

I am indebted to the many people I got to know within the perimeters of the Bethesda assisted-living community. Only a fraction of them are mentioned in my book, but they all fill my heart just the same.

My two daughters, Amanda and Allison, have been more important to this book than either of them knows. Many of the ideas in the story we have talked through together and in some instances experienced together.

A special thanks goes to Jessi Hoffman for her calm counsel and editorial genius, and to Peggy Nehmen for providing tremendous assistance with designing this book, for which I am extremely grateful.

Chapter 1

Her name was Audrey Margaret (Juengst) Hubele. I knew this wonderful lady as just "Mom." Her small, narrow house stood on a barely wooded and sparsely settled subdivision in the town of Concord Village, a suburb of St. Louis County, Missouri. The new roof had not yet attained the soft grey streaks of weather-beaten shingles. In daylight this house had a smooth-as-butter tint; by night it was the color of a grey cast-iron skillet. Built on top of a hill sloping sharply back from the street, it seemed to perch above the pavement, away from all the neighbors. If any wetness in the neighborhood arose, it never had a chance to reach her doors. The line of the front of the house was broken only by a porch with three steps, jutting forward like the blunt, swollen nose of a prizefighter. The backyard, the biggest in the neighborhood, opened to trees that surrounded the edges. The grounds looked like misplaced land from a state park.

When the house was built in 1956, my father requested that the contractor make sure the soil sloped away from the foundation to keep even the slightest chance of water out of the basement. When the worst floods in St. Louis caused the Mississippi, Missouri, and Meramec Rivers to overflow their banks in other parts of town, our house always stayed bone-dry. I remember one instance where my father and I were standing in the rain in the backyard. He drew with a stick in the mud to show me which direction the water was moving.

"Water can really do damage," said my father. "Water can ruin everything you own."

As a young boy, I only knew water as something all living things needed to survive. Water was the liquid we drank to quench our thirst. Drinking water from the garden hose was a treat on a hot summer day for any boy who lived in a house without air-conditioning and loved playing baseball during the summer. My early talks with my father about water flow were my first lessons in property management.

My father also told me he had planted the three oak trees in the backyard to keep the women in our house safe from the gaze of strangers, but mostly they were planted to soak up water and provide shade in the hot summer months. Besides, the only strangers seen walking behind our house were children who cut through the farmer's field to go play in the woods.

Over the backyard fence, a gravel road and the woods ran together for a few hundred yards, bordered by narrow rows of dirt, not yet ready for the tomato plant stakes used to help synthesize green sprouts whenever the fields decided haphazardly that they were ready for the change of season. The vista opened to another parcel of houses where a farmhouse and a barn once stood. The only things that remained were the memories of the big covered porch, windows boasting big blue shutters, and a copse of towering oak trees with massed limbs that spread in all directions like an octopus. Ivy crawled up the sunny side of the painted white main house and the roof, covered in copper shingles. Any flashes of remembering the details my childhood will always include the thickets of strawberry plants sprouted in clumps, hugging the ground in rows like a narrow carpeted hallway, positioned on the side of the farmer's barn a stone's throw from our home. Often in the summer when rays of sunlight lessened at the horizon, rabbits darted between the rows of foliage, lending the scenery a postcard-like ambience.

The years since my father died were a struggle for my mother. Because of her courage, she did her best to carry on and inspire others, but I knew she had a broken heart. No woman loved her man more than my mother loved my father. My father often told me how special my mother was, too. She never strayed from her morality in living her life, because she wanted her children to see her actions as good examples to emulate. Like she often said, "When the villains keep telling us lies, family is all we have left."

It was never clear what might happen in early spring in St. Louis, waiting for winter to end, the cold to ease, and the sun to welcome in the return of baseball season. Warm days raised hopes of attending to work that needed attention outside, but then one more deep snowfall might shut down the city again.

After shoveling snow in the driveway during one cold day in early March at Mom's house, I went inside and looked into the refrigerator to see what there was to eat. There was a pitcher of iced tea, but it probably had been there for a while ... a small plastic tub of stale lunch meat, possibly oven roasted chicken, and another package containing several slices of moldy Swiss cheese. Aligned inside the refrigerator door, there stood a host of squeeze bottles containing ketchup, mustard, honey, barbeque sauce, and various kinds of salad dressing. I poured out a gallon of skim milk that was seventeen days beyond its best-if-used-before date. I closed the refrigerator door, and instead of eating lunch, decided to lie down on the sofa in the living room and take a nap. Mom no longer lived in the house.

Lying there, I imagined my mother saying, "What good would it do you to eat that? You will get sick if you eat food kept on the shelf well beyond its expiration date." Mom always was looking out for her children. "Do the right thing, work hard, pay your dues, and everything will work out for you in the long run. Angels of your ancestors will guard you while you sleep," she would say.

As a young boy, I once asked Mom, "Why did God make you my mother?" She said, "God knew I would like you more than other kids' moms would like you." Once when I asked her, "What's for dinner?" She said, "We're having poison for dinner, and you're going to like it." It was her sense of humor that made spending time with Mom worth it.

I remember one time when I was very young; my mom sat on the sofa reading a book. Her feet were bare, and she was dressed in her bath robe. I was starting to notice all the bad news in newspapers and on the streets, and I worried my parents might die and leave me when I needed them most.

"Mom, are you and Dad going to die soon?" I asked.

"Honey, you shouldn't worry about such things," she answered. "Your father and I are going to live for a long time. She was trying to answer the best she could, but her words came in a broken pattern of gasps.

"My poor child," she began again. "Don't worry," she said, again breaking. "Have fun just being a kid."

"Okay," I said.

"Oh, honey," she said, grabbing and holding me close, not needing to tell me more. On the record player, she started playing an album full of Johnny Mathis songs to bring more happiness to the room, but it did little to change my thought process as the oldest child with three younger sisters. Two brothers in our neighborhood had already lost both of their parents, one due to cancer, and the other from a heart attack. I was too young to take care of other people, too young to care about anything too much. Being the young son of a mother who believed there could be a better world is in some ways harder than being the young son of a mother who never thinks about anything but the easy way of doing things.

Early on Mom tried to make me aware of the importance of telling the truth, sometimes pointing out that lies told by a president, governor, or any leader guiding a large group of people has an adverse effect on many. I remember her saying, "Nothing is free, and always speak the truth, because it is easier to memorize, and eventually you will need to rely on your recall." She taught me that false promises spread false hope. When a young boy is offered anything for free, it sounds like a good thing. But Mom tried her best to help me understand the irrelevance of government handouts and small, marginal free things, and to focus on my skills and my education. She often reminded me, "Education is the one thing no other person can take away from you." There was no way she was going to allow her only son to become anything like those men who legislated policy to keep themselves in control and to steal from others to line the pockets of their friends.

Raising her children, Mom was guarded, always keeping in mind her strong desire to practice fairness. At the end of the meal on Sunday evenings, once dessert dishes were set out, it was time for a special treat. She doled out two sweet rolls, bought from the local bakery, onto the plates of each child, going from the oldest to the youngest. Then she turned her attention to pouring four glasses of milk, this time reversing the order, starting with the youngest child.

When my father, George, first met Mom, working in Dr. Reuter's office in 1951, he was a cocky young man and she a dark-eyed beauty. That first year of dating was just a drop in the bucket compared to all the years they would spend together, but that year meant everything to Mom.

During the critical years of raising four children, there wasn't much time to think about herself, much less let her coffee get cold, so she daydreamed about all the fun she had going places on dates with George.

To bring back memories, I tried to get other family members to climb aboard for the treasure hunt of a lifetime. Find some remaining pieces of our family story, I begged, by helping me clean out the attic at Mom's house, so we'll have something to pass along to future generations. With no luck garnering help from either of my two daughters or my sisters (two of the sisters lived out of town), I began the adventure of going through Mom's attic by myself.

Somewhere in the attic, I knew I would find an account of the simpler life I remembered as a child, or at least life celebrated in a simpler way. Soon I was creeping up a ladder that I had brought up from the basement to take a look around the attic. Walking around and making sure to step on the old oak beams, I heard the old house creak with almost every movement I made. I figured the sounds were mostly a result of years of the house settling and big changes in temperatures in recent days. Within minutes, I found myself mired in stacks of things all around me. As I reached to grab onto an overhead beam for stability, a feeble breeze sprang up through the vent and vibrated the shadows of things stored in the unfinished attic. On afternoons during the dog days of a St. Louis summer, breathing is more difficult in attics void of windows and high in humidity. But on days any kind of breeze worked its way through the vents on either side of the house, it was a welcome sensation. Trailing the fingers of both my hands against the vertical beams for guidance, I took care to misstep on insulation, knowing this could cause a fall through the ceiling. Seven paces from the opening in the ceiling, where I entered the attic from the ladder, I spotted a box full of worthless family possessions, including two dented orange jack-o-lanterns, a set of yellow plastic drinking glasses, dusty bits and pieces of fake flower arrangements, and an old wooden baby bed, a walnut version at least fifty years old. That type of baby bed was deemed dangerous about three decades ago, due to an unusually high number of reported crib deaths.

I tried to reach past a smaller stack of junk quietly, but I knocked over a tin spaghetti strainer and an aluminum vegetable steamer that someone had given my parents for Christmas once. There was an excellent, brown, low-riding chair shaped like a catcher's mitt supported by a wire frame. Any unmarried male proclaiming himself a born-again hippie would love to have that in his bachelor pad. I set the chair aside, the start of a pile of things I would bring to Goodwill.

Outside the cold winter weather fast-forwarded to spring with cool rain and shameful winds the type that sometimes stripped asphalt shingles off roofs. At first, caught up in my work searching for something unexpected or surprising, I didn't notice the deteriorating weather until a fierce clap of thunder shattered my concentration. Then, looking out the vent on the attic's east end, I saw one of the neighbors down the street bringing in his trash cans and scurrying to get back under cover. At the end of another driveway, a round aluminum trash can lid went sailing, bouncing along on the pavement like a shiny silver ball ricocheting off bumpers inside a pinball machine. For several minutes the rain pelted down so hard that it almost obscured the staccato bursts of lightning flashing in the sky to the south and east. No worries, I was inside, protected from the elements.

There was an old portmanteau, left alone in the attic like an old Rambler in a salvage yard, packed with old silk dresses and yellowed sweaters inside both inner compartments. The portmanteau was made of thick tan leather, and red metal hardware encased all the edges, tightly holding the memories of trips long ago. After moving a lot of junk, including old paint cans, two empty oil cans, a non-functional stationary bike, and a cracked wastebasket out of the way, I opened up the door of an antique wardrobe chest made from cedar. It looked heavy, awkward, and worn. Sitting on the top shelf was a framed piece of paper documenting a physical exam rendering treatment to George Hubele, my father, and stating that a report was sent to the company he was applying to for work, the Seven-Up Bottling Company. My life began as the gleam in the eye of a hopeful Seven-Up Bottling Company employee who was in for a physical screening but ended up marrying the nurse who had scheduled his appointment. This had to be the report that resulted from the exam during which Father met Mother. They had framed it as a memento of the day they met. I was touched.

I thought about my parents, and how they had been when they were young. Mom, as a girl, had a gift for English and math, so her first job, helping Monsignor Rogers at her parish, entailed not only phone answering and meal serving but also doing business calculations and handling office files. By the time she finished high school and World War II ended, she was keeping all the parish books, reading the mail, and organizing the receipts for the figuring taxes. Already two men had proposed to her, each of them good song-and-dance men, but Mom intended to live an intellectual, moral, and happy life, with a different kind of man, a man of substance.

When she became a nurse, Mom found magic working for Dr. Reuter, the general practitioner who administered the physical Dad needed to gain employment at the Seven-Up Bottling Company. To get to Dr. Reuter's office, a patient needed to walk or drive to Ninth and Montgomery Street, one block west of Broadway in the north section of St. Louis. A patient then walked up a long flight of stairs to reach the doctor's office. On April 18, 1952, my parents—Audrey and George—met. He barely opened his mouth, but surprised her with his deep, down-to-earth voice. She felt her stomach flutter.

"Hi, I'm George. I need a physical exam for a new job," said the young man. He had a face created to steal a woman's breath and haunt her dreams. To her, perhaps, his looks were as close to perfection as nature would allow. His eyes of laser blue enhanced his knowing smile beneath his froth of thick, curly blond hair.

"I'm Audrey, Dr. Reuter's nurse and assistant," said Audrey, trying hard not to reveal how overwhelmed he made her feel. "Have a seat in the examination room, the first door on the right. Fill out this form and the doctor will be in to see you in a few minutes."

"Will you come back and talk to me, to check if I have questions, or want to ask for your phone number?" teased George.

"I have lots of other things to do right now," said Audrey. "Dr. Reuter will address any of your questions."

"At least tell me your last name," insisted George.

"My name is Audrey Juengst."

"Do you live around here?" he pressed.

"On Warren Street, near where it intersects with St. Louis Avenue."

She had the impression that George's world was ordered by integrity and trust, that he understood integrity even though he was brash. He wasn't preoccupied with pretending to be something he wasn't, and his sexy blue eyes signaled he was adventurous and fun. He looked like a man who could laugh easily if something was genuinely funny. By telling him she lived on Warren Street, she figured he could ask the telephone operator for her number if he wanted it.

Helping run the doctor's office had given Audrey experience in dealing with the cool macho dudes of the world. Many of them could be brought into compliance with a smile and notice of a professional badge displayed on a nurse's uniform. Not backing down helped, too. Though the first impression George made was "cool macho," Audrey could see there was something beneath the surface. Her heart fluttered for the man she had just met, but her excitement at their meeting was about to be put on hold.

Twenty minutes after her encounter with George, another man came walking up the stairs, holding his own severed left arm in his right hand, his clothes covered in blood. Audrey was standing face-to-face with a man bleeding to death. The doctor's office was about to be thrown into turmoil, the severely injured man still alive, and standing at the top of the stairs. Early on in her career, Audrey had learned never to let her feelings get in the way of doing her job, but this day was becoming increasingly more difficult, the highs and the lows, than that of any other day in her life to date. Determined to meet the doctor's expectations of her, she hollered at the top of her voice, nearly shaking the building.

"Doctor, come fast. We have an emergency!" she yelled.

"Audrey, what's wrong? I'm on my way," Dr. Reuter called back.

About eight seconds passed before the doctor appeared, but the seconds seemed like hours. The event unfolded quickly. The injured man may have sensed his life was over. Maybe he figured he had already lost too much blood and lacked the energy to endure anything more. Maybe all his sensory receptors were overloaded with confusion and he was simply in shock. Whatever the reason, before the doctor could get to him, the injured man walked back down the stairs and out the front door of the building. He staggered a few more paces to the familiar interior surrounding of his car parked in the street, where he died instantly. Dr. Reuter and Nurse Audrey frantically ran to the injured man's car to apply pressure at the site of the amputation, but it was too late; he was gone.

That evening, after the doors to the doctor's office were locked and the day's heat had dissipated, a disturbance blew in from the west, and the black sky unleashed a fury that drenched the city. It was the kind of weather that made it easy for a young woman to sit in her room and think and reflect. Audrey would never forget about the dying man, but she couldn't stop thinking about George, either. She thought he could be the man she could love with all her heart. She had been intrigued by his bold manner that suggested he had an adventurous side. He seemed to live an edgy existence beyond the scope of her limited, girl-next-door experience. She hoped he would call and ask her on a date. When he did, a week later, she said yes. When he arrived to pick her up, he introduced himself to her father. And when he walked her outside to where his car was parked, he opened the passenger door for her, like a gentleman. She sat happily beside him, quiet and unperturbed, riding in the car. That would be the way she would ride with him for all fifty-two years that they would be together, keeping watch on the passing scenery outside the window, the big oaks and the patches of dirt, the manicured fresh-smelling lawns, and the newly discovered buildings seen for the first time. She was really a backup alert system in case of reckless drivers behaving badly or an animal crossing the road at the wrong moment, and George grew to rely on the admonitions of his "co-pilot."

Even years later, the mere thought of the dying man on the day she met George made bile well up in an indigestible burn at the back of Audrey's esophagus. This one moment affected how she approached doing her job for the rest of her life. She was hard on herself, but in reality, nothing she could have done would have changed the outcome of that situation. The experience did make her strive for excellence in every situation she encountered as a nurse and mother afterwards.

My reminiscing ended, and I carefully put the framed document aside to take home. My thoughts returned to the present—my aging mother in an assisted living facility, fighting hard to stay healthy and positive. After fighting serious illnesses later in life, she had grown barely able to care for herself. How she hated giving up any of her independence. She fought me for weeks when it was time to take away the car keys, and she fought the idea of moving away from the house she raised her four children in and lived in for sixty years. Moving meant she had to pare down a lifetime of belongings, leaving behind an old house with memories and fifteen-hundred square feet of comfortable living space, and moving to an apartment one-fifth that size. Giving up her cane for a wheelchair was a battle, too. It didn't matter that she didn't need to go out much. At this point in her life, she struggled to find enough energy just to buy groceries.

Five years after Mom's major heart surgery, my sister Kathy and I decided to visit Bethesda, an assisted living facility in St. Louis County that we had been told by a social worker was very good. Mom needed more than just help with managing daily activities. She needed a personalized care plan and a certified nursing staff readily available to assist her with rehabilitation, therapy, shots, and keeping track of medications.

Because symptoms of fatigue and rapid heartbeat had become more evident, Mom's second heart surgeon, Dr. Carey, had been hopeful a procedure called "cardiac ablation" would help. Approximately three-million American adults have been diagnosed with atrial fibrillation (a-fib), while another three million don't even know they have it. Most people suffering from this condition describe their symptoms as a sudden fluttering in their chest and being out of breath. For some patients, medications can control rhythmic conditions and regulate a racing heart. Unfortunately for Mom, probably due to her lifelong diabetic condition and living with one artificial valve already, anti-arrhythmic drugs made her groggy, lethargic, and barely able to function. The relatively new procedure of cardiac ablation ended up as the best option for her. Instead of opening up her heart again, the fix was done by her surgeon threading catheters, with electrodes on the ends, from a blood vessel in her groin up into her heart under x-ray guidance. Then Dr. Carey used extreme cold to freeze off scar tissue that was causing her irregular heartbeats. After the surgery and two more days of monitoring in the hospital, Mom was ready for a rehab facility, and Bethesda seemed like a good possibility, perhaps even for the long term.

Seeing the grounds at Bethesda for the first time, any visiting relative would find the vast array to be much more than just a plain residential setting. Surrounded by formal gardens, it occupied a prime spot off Telegraph Road, just a few blocks away from a privileged stretch of land with some three-hundred businesses and shops, and a long jog from the rolling hills and deeply indented banks of the Mississippi River. The dining room could seat two hundred. Only a few of Missouri's wealthiest families—the Buschs, the Danforths, the McDonnells, the Pulitzers, the Kroenkes, the Knights, and the Taylors—had estates more immensely grandiose than Bethesda.

We've all done this: judge a person or a place the first time we lay eyes on them. Before any experience even begins, we start deciding whether we will be returning for another visit. The connection between appearance and satisfaction with service does not go unnoticed by eldercare facilities. Most establishments are careful to have a beautiful front lobby to create a warm and friendly first impression. But the residents spend less than one percent of their time in the lobby. We wanted to find out if enough focus and support was geared toward the areas where the residents spent most of their time.

We decided we wanted to see what the inside of the apartments looked like, to talk to the business manager, to observe the nurses, and to find out more about patient care. Would this be a place Mom would like, or just a place that looked comfortable on the surface?

Kathy and I met with Sarita, the business office manager at Bethesda. She offered us a tour of the facility.

We walked past an upscale dining area where a sign stated the times when meals were served each day. Sarita pointed out the location of the on-site beauty- and barber shop. We stopped at a café stocked with free beverages and snacks for residents and their visitors. A nice-sized library with shelves full of bestsellers, and tables with laptops for Internet access, was situated thirty feet from the elevator on the second floor. We gazed past the activities room, where a group of seniors were engaged in what appeared to be board games, administered by a male who looked to be high school age and wearing a volunteer's badge.

Sarita told us about the history of Bethesda. Older than penicillin, it was founded in 1889 by Roger and Elizabeth Hayne. With the help of a Dr. Edward Saunders, and they opened Bethesda as a home to care for abandoned infants, unwed mothers, and elderly women suffering from the devastating ailments of the day.

"I suspect the original location was in the downtown area of the city somewhere," said Kathy.

"It's said that the three founders pooled their resources and started with forty dollars to start their work," said Sarita.

"Bethesda has come a long way," I commented.

"Today, we have five retirement communities, all located in different area suburbs of St. Louis."

"What a difference a hundred and twenty-five years makes!" said Kathy.

Sarita went on to tell us about all the community services offered by Bethesda today, including skilled nursing assistance, memory care, rehab, therapy, home health aid, respite and hospice care, and help finding senior solutions for everyday needs.

"I know housekeeping, cooking meals, and keeping up with medications has become increasingly difficult for our mother," said Kathy.

"When life is crazy, it's good for our residents to take time to do something that relaxes them," said Sarita. "Games, puzzles, ceramics, painting, sewing, knitting, and arts and crafts are all options for resident. They're usually able to find something that strikes their fancy. The activities room is here so residents can create personalized things rather than go out and spend money on the same items."

"I like the music playing in the background," I said.

"Music is usually playing in the activities room during the day," Sarita said with a smile. "Music speaks to the inner child. So do painting and drawing. But perhaps the most direct route to a person's heart is through a story or a game. People from all cultures have understood this for hundreds of years."

The tour continued through the living area, which

featured forty-eight spacious, private, assisted-living apartments, each with its own bathroom and shower. Outside each doorway, flat touch-screen computers for tracking medical records were mounted on the hallway walls. The apartments were connected to a central hallway, creating a kind of web that made me think of a neighborhood all under one roof.

"Therapy is administered in our exercise room and spa," Sarita explained, as we passed by that section of the facility.

"Our mother wears a pacemaker, so the spa is a no-no for her," I said.

"That's something that we would add to her chart," said Sarita.

Sarita invited us to explore on our own and said she'd be in her office if we had more questions. Kathy and I walked down the hall and opened the door to an empty, unlocked apartment. The small kitchen didn't provide much space for anything, but there were still plenty of possibilities. The cabinets and countertop would definitely keep the kitchen space from looking cluttered, while faux-brick backsplash tiles and stainless steel faucets added charm. A deep-beige painted wall united the kitchen to the living room as an accent wall.

"One of the keys to decorating smaller spaces is to use fewer pieces," said my sister. "One large framed piece of artwork would look nice on this accent wall."

"Yes it would," I said, as if I was an expert on the subject of decorating.

"We need to help Mom understand there's no despair in downsizing. She'd have way less housecleaning, and she wouldn't have to worry about her meds anymore. With a little creativity and the right pieces of furniture, she might end up liking this cozy space more than her house," said Kathy.

"Mom is good at making new friends," I said. "She's clever enough to find new ways to make old habits fit into the way she would live here."

"It's hard to see her staying lonely for long in this place," Kathy agreed.

Thoughts were swishing about in my brain, overwhelming the part that has to decide where to even start.

"Mom has lived in her house for nearly sixty years and she knows where to find her stuff. Moving means leaving some of the memories at the old house," I said. But Kathy, being a nurse, had experience with things like this I lacked.

"The elderly tend to compensate well," she pointed out, "because they've been doing it for a while. I think Mom would do beautifully here," she said with a pleased smile. "Look, there are even safety rails in the bathroom."

"I've seen enough," I said. "I don't think we need to drive anywhere else."

Kathy agreed. We went to find Sarita.

"We have two openings right now, but the assisted living apartments fill fast," Sarita explained as she seated us inside her office. "If you want one of the apartments, you need to let me know as soon as possible, probably within the next week," said Sarita.

"We love the place," said Kathy, "but we'll have to talk with Mom before we commit."

Sarita explained what paperwork would be needed and how the finances would work. I figured Mom had enough money to live at Bethesda for one year if her health held out that long, before some kind of new arrangement would have to be made.

"At some point, if a resident's money runs out, what happens?" I asked.

"We won't kick a resident out to the curb," Sarita answered. "We work with Medicare and the family to find a reasonable solution. Corporate and private donations help to keep costs down some."

Chapter 2

The next afternoon Mom decided (after a long discussion with her doctor, the hospital social worker, Kathy, and me) that it was best to go straight to Bethesda from the hospital to start rehabilitation, and then to move to an assisted living unit when rehab was complete. She was sure she would break down if we went back to her house in the interim. I called Sarita, made an appointment, and signed Mom up to live at Bethesda.

The first day Mom spent at Bethesda, she acquainted herself with her new surroundings and got to know her new neighbors. I visited the next evening to find out how things were going for her. The front door to her apartment was wide open.

"Just a minute," she called on hearing my voice. "I washed my hair, and its wet and dripping." She walked into the living room, a towel swathed around her head.

"Somewhere in this world, people must act normal. It's as if my world wasn't crazy enough when I lived in my old house," said Mom.

"Most of the things you own and use are here now," I said. "And you have a brand-new, high-definition TV in your apartment. No one wants to go back to the days where neighbors had to share telephone party lines and families had little choice but to watch network shows aired by two or three channels on black-and-white TVs."

"I lived through twelve presidential administrations, listening to the news on the radio, and then watching it in black-and-white, then color," said Mom. "I raised all my children in my old house. I miss it."

"I know you do. You and Dad sacrificed so your children would have more than you both had as youngsters," I said. "Remember when we used to sit at the kitchen table on Saturday nights and play board games?"

"Yes, of course. I was comfortable in my old house," said Mom. "I have lots of memories of you and your sisters running around in the backyard, playing and laughing."

As children, we are lucky if we live in a house where memories are made of our own volition and our parents are kind. Ours was such a house.

"Your apartment is modern and nicely furnished," I said, trying to focus Mom on the positives. "The cooks here will make all your meals for you. Won't that be nice? Give it some time. Moving is a big adjustment."

"How did I end up here?" asked Mom.

I just looked at her.

"Now I have to deal with all these eccentric people who roam the halls and talk to extra-terrestrials through their Styrofoam coffee cups," she muttered.

"That's funny. But now you have nurses to give you your shots and your meds."

"I was worried about someone else giving me my insulin shots, but the nurse stuck the needle in my midsection like I was the Pillsbury dough boy's sister. I didn't feel a thing."

"That's good," I said, hoping the conversation was headed in a cheerful direction. "The nurses are just trying to keep the residents healthy and safe."

"I tried to take a nap, but they came in and woke me. I wish they would let me to sleep, especially when I'm having a good dream."

"What were you dreaming about?" I asked.

"Other residents were offering me one-hundred dollars for each container of ice cream I had stockpiled in my refrigerator. But then a nurse woke me up before I ever collected a dime," said Mom, removing the towel from her head. Her wavy grey hair was medium-length, cut straight around, on a line just two centimeters below the lobes of her ears. She tossed her head now, like a pony shaking its mane.

"What can I do to make you more comfortable here?" I asked. Mom didn't say anything. "You should probably decide before we both get senile."

"Who are you saying is senile?" asked Mom.

"I forget where I set things as much as you do. Let's just say we share equal amounts of senility," I said.

"To answer your question, just keep visiting whenever you can. That will help me forget about my separation from home and make it more bearable." Mom looked so sad.

"I will keep visiting," I said.

"There are people here to talk with, but they're all strangers."

"You'll make friends. You've always been good at that. And Kathy and I will come by to visit almost every day."

I thought about all the times, when I was a kid that Mom drove across town when one of us was sick because she wanted us to receive care from Dr. Eto, one of the best pediatricians in St. Louis. She drove us to our ball games, and stayed to watch and cheer us on. She drove us back and forth to our part-time jobs in all kinds of weather, before we were old enough to drive ourselves. When we had to have a new pair of athletic shoes or a certain crazy clothing item that was in style, she drove us to the stores that stocked what we wanted until we found something that fit. Now, in a reversal of roles, I would drive to go visit her. I knew how much it meant to her to receive my support.

My mother had been the kind of mom who treated her children respectfully, not like some who insist that their children ask for approval each time they open their mouths. Mom was a good listener and was genuinely interested in what others, including children, had to say. She was also good at admonishing us in a tactful, respectful way. The directive would usually begin with, "I understand why you feel that way, but ..." "I understand why you feel that way about wanting more independence, but your little sisters need circumvention to help them grow. Now go help them clean up their room, and take out the trash after that," I remember her telling me on more than one occasion. "I understand why you feel that way, but your sister was only trying to help when she shrunk your baseball uniform in the dryer." "I understand why you feel that way, but you had the first year of your life all to yourself, and you never had to share anything. Your sisters have always had to share things. Now that you have a driver's license, take them to the store and let them buy their school supplies. Here's twenty dollars. You should have enough change left to stop at the grocery store on the way home and buy a gallon of milk." Mom was gentle and kind, but she always got across her point.

As a new resident at Bethesda, Mom was anxious, but when after five days she moved from the rehab section of the facility to her new apartment, she started to feel more comfortable. She started to warm to a new friend named Virginia, who was outgoing and lived across the hall. On the days when Mom felt better, her smile widened and her dimples ballooned inwards, her whole body reflecting an attitude of such engagement that others couldn't fail to notice her. It was easy for her to make friends. People had always been drawn to her, though she was probably completely unaware of how her dazzling facial expressions transformed her words in moments she talked to strangers.

There was one glaring thing about the kitchen in Mom's new apartment that was different from the kitchen in her old house. Her apartment kitchen didn't have a stove. It had a microwave to heat snacks, but her meals were served to her in the dining hall. Residents were forever talking about what American, Italian, Polish, and German foods they liked and what a wonderful thing it was to live the last phase of their lives not having to cook. The cooks at Bethesda kept trying new things, and the residents kept on critiquing the food whether they ate it or not. I stayed to eat dinner one night that first week, with Mom and Virginia.

"What do you think of the Polish sausage?" asked Mom.

"I think it's overcooked," said Virginia.

Virginia, like Mom, was the type of person who always counted the chess pieces, before putting them away in the original cardboard box. She made certain all the pieces were there for whoever was going to play the board game next.

"I think I'll just have an ice cream cone for dinner tonight," said Mom.

"You're only having dessert?" asked Virginia.

"I'm not that hungry," said Mom.

"Well, I'm hungry. I'm eating whatever is served," I said.

"Steve, did you know the ice cream cone was invented in St. Louis?" asked Virginia.

"I think I heard something about that. Wasn't ravioli invented in St. Louis, too?"

"Both food items were big hits at the World's Fair in St. Louis in 1904," said Virginia. "When an ice cream vendor ran out of cups, he asked a waffle vendor to help by rolling up waffles to hold ice cream. Of course your mother and I heard lots of stories about the World's Fair from our aunts and uncles and grandparents."

"When we were little girls, during the Depression years, ice cream cones were seldom eaten by anybody, except on very special occasions," said Mom.

"This potato salad is good," said Virginia.

"Take a bite of the potato salad Mom," I said.

"Try it to see if you like it Audrey. Sometimes we make the mistake of eating with our eyes," said Virginia.

"Can I hold my nose if I don't like it?" asked Mom.

After trying only one bite, she said, "My potato salad is better. When I made it for my husband and children, I made it from scratch. My husband said my potato salad was his favorite dish."

Next Mom took a stab at a morsel of a buttery topped grouping of Brussels sprouts. But the Brussels sprouts wouldn't do either.

"These have the texture of dried mud on a shoe sole," said Mom.

I remembered when as a little boy pushing certain vegetables to the edge of my plate. While my old boyish habit of eating everything on the plate one item at a time had evolved into something more sophisticated, the parent-child relationship with respect to my mother and food seemed now to be playing out in reverse.

The cooks at Bethesda had to have thick skins and a strong willingness to please their customers; otherwise the residents' complaints could be hurtful if they took them to heart.

As Virginia ate her potato salad, I munched on breadsticks and garden salad made with leaf lettuce, carrots,
celery, tomatoes, boiled egg, some kind of tiny beans, and
topped with croutons and grated cheese. Then plates of
spaghetti and meatballs with were served as the main
course. Mom did decide to eat two breadsticks.

"Lots of different foods are mentioned in the Bible, and
now we understand them to be essential to our health,"
said Mom.

"That's right," said Virginia. "Olive oil was a kitchen
staple in Jesus's time. Not only was it used for cooking, but
as hair conditioner, lamp fuel, and to make soap."

"Beans and lentils provided protein to ancient families
when meat was scarce," said Mom.

"There was no such thing as processed white flour
during Biblical days. Probably without even knowing it,
people kept their blood pressure down by filling their bel-
lies with bread made from crushed whole grains," Virginia
added.

"Does the Bible mention at what age a person should
start eating prunes?" I asked, but didn't get the reaction I
hoped for from my dinner companions.

As the days passed, Mom began to associate more with
Virginia because she had a similar sense of humor. Mom
also began to eat more of the selections at meal times.

For two weeks, Kathy and I visited Mom every day at
rehab, hoping we were helping her adjust to a new living
arrangement. Some days we visited her in her room. Other
days we went to therapy with her. She was very weak.

Her face was swollen. She shuffled when she walked, and she could barely lift her arms over her head. While she was busy working with one of the physical therapists learning exercises to strengthen the leg muscles necessary to lift her feet, Kathy and I would grab five- and ten-pound dumbbells and do sets of biceps and forearm curls to help pass the time. We were lifting small weights and participating in the specialized exercises together as a family.

"It is always better for our residents to take small steps when trying to improve their gait, better than shuffling along or trying to run too fast," said Lisa, a medical coordinator in charge of the rehab facility, as she walked by Virginia and Mom.

"Mom, are you listening to Lisa?" I asked.

"The human body is a sophisticated engine that requires proper care, just like a car needs routine maintenance checks to run properly," said Lisa. "Life is more enjoyable when you have the energy to embrace the day."

"This sounds a little over the top to me," Mom whispered.

"Give it a chance," I said.

"Our days of training for a marathon or bicycling in a long race are over. But we can still lift light weights, do chair exercises, improve the way we walk, and maintain a healthy routine," said Lisa.

"Somehow, I wish all this exercising would prepare me to play golf again," said Mom.

Music played in the background, and pausing only to get the rhythm in her mind, Mom lifted her left foot, bent her leg at the knee and pointed her toes down toward the floor. Then she repeated the same steps with her right leg. "One, two, three, and hold on the left, change; one, two, three, and hold on the right," said the physical therapist as Mom went through this procedure. The savory tune was stimulating. Mom's mood lifted as her breath shortened, and the exhilaration that always fills a person during a workout began to surge in her.

"Now slide your feet apart and put your hands on your hips," said the therapist. "Now bend to the left, come back up, and bend to the right."

It was several years since Mom had played golf or taken any long walks at the mall. She was having trouble keeping pace, like a flutist who is off-key with the other musicians in the orchestra. You might figure she would feel ridiculous doing such simple exercises with so much effort, but Mom did not care what she looked like to anybody. In her mind, she focused on getting strong, and despite her aging muscles and damaged heart, she displayed elegance, dignity, and coordination.

The physical therapists ran a tight ship. They had a job to do. Because they consulted with the residents' doctors, they kept charts and designed specialized plans to target weaknesses in hopes of helping their patients increase their mobility. To them, doing exercises improperly was simply unacceptable. They kept a close eye on the patients to make sure they were doing them right the entire length of their sessions.

Each day during her physical therapy routine, Mom felt a little better. After a while, I noticed that instead of shuffling her feet when she walked, Mom was taking small steps with the help of her walker. Instead of staying in her room, she was getting about, discovering some of the features of Bethesda. I felt so proud of her. Mom always had resilience, an ability to cultivate a kind of transcendence, even in dangerous-health circumstances. Now she was regularly visiting and talking to other residents. Watching her made me profoundly grateful for everything she had, of which material things counted very little. We were both becoming sharply aware of how to react in situations beyond our control that could shift from something good to something uncertain or dangerous at a moment's notice.

When I walked into her apartment on my next visit to check on Mom, she was sitting with her head bowed in the darkness and her eyes closed. Interesting how eager she was to carry on alone, how adamantly she would clear the room when she was tired, but secretly hoped someone would visit and wake her later. She wanted that someone, that link, to forge on with when she opened her eyes. It was me she wanted as her beacon when she was receiving mixed signals.

"Busy week?" Mom asked as she woke from her dozing, hearing me try to quietly shut her apartment door.

"Yes. I can't remember the last time I had a whole day to just do nothing," I said.

"I know what you mean. I wish your Dad was still

alive and he and I could spend an entire weekend together, that's all," Mom said, dabbing at her eyes. "It's like I'm living through the same pain over and over. One thing had troubled Mom and Dad's relationship, and that was his need to be gone at work many hours a week. It seemed Mom now was feeling neglected—I hadn't been to visit in days—and that was stirring up her memories of feeling neglected by Dad.

"Mom, I'm sorry things are so hard for you right now," I said.

"It's been eight years since your father died. I haven't forgotten him, you know," Mom said, twisting the wedding ring she still wore on her finger.

"I haven't forgotten him either. Dad put in plenty of hours working to earn enough to take care of the house and our family," I said.

"Nobody called or visited me the last three days. I guess everybody wants to stay out of harm's way," Mom said.

She stood up, shuffled across the room, and sat down heavily at the end of her couch closest to the window. Sadness surrounded her, an emptiness she usually escaped, because her sister Rose would call or her friend Helen would visit to cheer her mood and encourage her to fight for more joy in life. But for her now, it had been far too long since anyone had sent out an inquiry about her existence. She hated when too many hours flashed by without a relative or a close friend checking on her. She worried whether other people were just too busy, just didn't care, or was something seriously wrong? Maybe they were catching up with the mail, paying the bills, working, or running errands. But not knowing the real reason why no one had called just added to her worrying.

By now I was gearing up to deliver a heated response, one that would explain how someone had to work to pay the bills, but something held me back. I knew Mom's outburst had far less to do with me working and not setting aside enough time to visit than it did with all the things attacking her quality of life. Her eyes suddenly filled with tears, and she plucked a tissue from a nearby box of Kleenex. I reminded myself that a person is a fool to take a few carelessly chosen and misdirected words seriously, because a situation only worsens when remarks provoke a person into losing their temper. And there I was, stopping to think—glad I wasn't going to have to look back and wonder why something stupid I said caused something stupid to happen.

When my father died of cancer, his death was an experience that helped me realize several truths on a number of levels. Everybody knows they're going to die eventually, but most people still try to fool their selves about death, walking around in life half-asleep. The truth is that once you watch a loved one fight a deliberating disease, staying strong to the end even when they realize their death is eminent, you learn how you are supposed to live. It is profound thing to realize we are learning the right way to live by watching a courageous family member die. With the death of a parent, we evaluate our own lives, and where we are headed. Something hard to explain happens, something much bigger and different than an ordinary experience.

"I just wish we could go back to happier times. How'd I end up here?" said Mom.

"I know all these changes have been difficult for you, Mom," I said, no longer feeling anger but genuine compassion. "Let's just enjoy our visit together. Some things we have to leave in God's hands. I'll stay as long as I can today, but I have to work tonight, and I'll be back in two days to check on you."

"God can see all; I'll keep comfort in knowing that God sees me," said Mom.

Seeing Mom dissolve into tears of sadness was an uncommon experience for me. Showing this much emotion was somewhat unprecedented for her, as usually she was able to fight back against misfortune. Now, after losing her husband, losing her health, losing her car keys, losing her house, and losing so many freedoms she had taken for granted her entire life, she was finding it all a challenging adjustment. Just getting around was difficult.

I handed Mom a bag I had been carrying.

"What's this? It isn't my birthday," said Mom.

"Open it," I said, smiling.

Earlier in the week, I had dropped off a box of donations at the Goodwill store near my house. I decided to walk around inside the store and shop for a comfortable pair of shoes for Mom. She wore a size-seven normally, but her feet often swelled because of her diabetic condition, I hoped to find a comfortable pair of shoes for her that was one size bigger than the shoes she had stored in her closet. All the shoes she wore had rough places inside that rubbed the knuckles on her toes and chafed the backs of her heels on both feet. I nearly jumped for joy when I discovered an almost brand-new pair of size-eight light-blue orthopedic tennis shoes resting on a shelf and priced at only eight dollars. I bought them, drove to another store at the mall, and bought a new pair of white cotton socks, the low-ankle-cut kind mostly worn by women. I was hoping my small gesture would not only cheer her up but make walking easier.

"Wow! New tennis shoes. I love the color," she said. "Are they size-seven-swollen?"

"Try them on," I said. "Put your new socks on first. I'll help you."

After tying the laces on her new tennis shoes, Mom stood up from her chair.

"They're comfortable," she said. "Maybe I'll enter the Senior Olympics."

"What distance would you train for if I signed you up?" I teased.

"The shortest distance," she joked back.

"Probably fifty meters, then," I said. "I could help you practice your form running, or maybe you could learn to throw the shot put or discuss with a few simple instructions."

"Don't you have to spin around, and bend, and lunge to throw those objects?"

"Yes," I said. "We could practice out by the garden."

"Well, that would give all the residents quite a laugh. We are in no need of people laughing at us in the garden. Laughing with us, yes, but not at us. I think my new shoes were meant for walking."

"Maybe I should've bought you a new pair of boots," I said.

"No, these tennis shoes are just fine. The socks are the perfect thickness. Thank you very much," Mom said with a smile, looking much more cheerful than she had when I walked in. I think it meant something to her, knowing that even though I hadn't come for visit for several days, I had managed to find time to go shopping for her.

"I found my old pair of wooden shoe trees in the back of my bedroom closet at the old house," I said. "I stuck them in your new tennis shoes to help stretch them."

"You brought those shoe trees home from Wolff's Clothiers when you were a shoe salesman, right?" she asked.

"Yes, you remember. I worked in the shoe department on weekends my last two years of high school. I sold Freeman shoes, a high-end brand for men that was manufactured in New York City back then."

"The shoes were expensive, but they were well made. I remember a pair your father bought lasted a long time."

"My boss told me to tell customers that most of the brands by this manufacturer were made from calfskin leather, which was a fact," I said. "We sold shoes made from alligator and sea-turtle hides too, before anyone paid attention to the treatment of wild animals or endangered species lists."

"Today, if you told customers anything was made of calfskin," said Mom, "they would probably be upset, picturing some man killing a calf behind a barn, before the creature even had a chance to live."

"But if you tell customers, like shoe salespeople do today, that the shoes they want to buy are made from cowhide, they imagine the old cow had a good life and died of natural causes, and like a person whose organs are donated after their death, the old cow's hide goes to a good cause," I said.

Mom chuckled. "Well, it's all a matter of how you market a thing, I guess. I think my new shoes and socks will bring some comfort to my swollen feet, and they are made from cotton fabric, not calfskin or cowhide. Let's take a little walk and try them out."

Because a freight worker had the elevator delayed at ground level, we started down the hall toward the stairs. I walked in front, while Mom kept one hand on the banister and the other in a belt loop at my waist, all the way down the stairwell. Once we were down to the last step and the exit door to the garden was within our sight, Mom let go with both hands and jumped from the bottom step, landing unsteadily, but regaining her footing in the open threshold. She began to laugh, her eyes wide open.

"What if you had slipped and broken your leg or hip?" I asked.

"I have doctors. Compared to the operations I've been through, getting a cast on me or a pin in me would be a walk in the park," said Mom. "That one small jump took me back to my childhood, when I played hopscotch with my sisters. Even an old woman needs a little excitement from time to time. Life has to stay interesting."

"Mom, I do give you credit for your positive attitude, but please walk more carefully around this building," I said.

Perhaps my mother was reverting back to her childhood, or maybe she was acting like a child who pretends and enjoys making up a game to play. But nothing about her nature included enough mischief to purposefully hurt herself or someone else. Though neither of us needed any additional mishaps, especially preventable ones, I let any more talk about the incident slide. Mom would never forgive me if she thought I was treating her like a child. I was her son. *I* was supposed to listen to *her*.

"Now that we've made it to the garden, I have a sudden desire to run away," said Mom. "Whatever direction we go is no matter to me. You pick the direction. I'll go north, south, west, or east."

"Are we walking, hitch-hiking, or taking my truck?" I asked, playing along.

"We might not get very far if we walk," said Mom.

"We might make it to the end of the parking lot. Then we could point our thumbs up in the air and hope someone driving along the road will give us a ride."

"No, hitch-hiking is a bad idea," Mom answered. "You see very few hitch-hikers on the side of the road these days because it's become too dangerous. I like riding in your truck."

The afternoon was peaceful, with the sunlight filtering in on the garden through the trees, like it was staggering in from half-closed blinds in a large window. Mom and I liked imagining that either of us could run away on a whim, and while talking about it helped satisfy secret desires, we both understood that it was just a fantasy.

"It looks like the elevator is available now. Maybe we should ride it back upstairs," I said, "because we still have the long walk down the hall to get back to your apartment."

"You're right. I'm getting thirsty anyway. We can run away or take a ride at another time," said Mom. "When we get back, I'll pour a glass of ice water for both of us."

Back at the apartment, as Mom got our drinks, I noticed how saggy the skin on her arms had become. Freckles, bruises, and liver spots dotted her veined hands and arms like a state map's worth of recognized towns. But Mom's up mood was continuing, and now she wanted to talk politics.

"I wish the politicians would stop wasting time and taxpayers' money," she said. "I pray, 'Dear God, please help me, and reform all of those idiots, too.' I'm hoping my prayers help, because nothing else is working. It's a wonder these politicians are even capable of dressing themselves in the morning, because paying attention to details or doing real work seems to be beyond them."

"It's funny hearing that from the mouth of a woman who just moved to an assisted living apartment," I said.

"I guess that is kind of funny," said Mom.

Mothers like her, when she was young and healthy,

made sure their children finished homework before they were allowed to play or eat dinner or watch TV. Children were taught discipline and told to complete the task before reaping the reward. "Ifs" and "buts" were not accepted by these mothers when their children made up excuses to avoid attending to their responsibilities, homework and chores. The children needed to do their part, because mothers like her were busy cooking three meals a day, reading to their kids, nursing them in sickness, scrubbing the kitchen floor, washing the bed linens, ironing clothes, and watching the evening news to stay informed about current events.

"I've arrived at a point where I can't stand listening to the president's press secretary anymore," Mom said. "How stupid does he think people are? His job is to tell Americans the truth about current affairs, but the man holding the position is told to lie and doctor the truth so it sounds the way they'd like it to sound," said Mom. "A good mother tells her children what they need to hear, not what they want to hear, and a good press secretary should tell the truth to the public, not spin words about failed policies, especially when it's obvious that something has gotten worse."

"Our government was not set up to stonewall the American public at every turn," I said.

In so many ways, Mom's mind was still sharp. She had strong opinions, especially about politics. But in recent years, she had started to suffer some degree of short-term memory loss, and sometimes, in talking, she would get confused. At the same time, she amazed me in her ability to retell stories ingrained into her mind many years ago. She had lived through five wars, fifteen presidential administrations, hundreds of new laws and regulations, and had followed politics with great interest since she was a teenager. Now her recounting of events was easier in the morning, before fatigue stuck a blow in late afternoon, a phenomenon the nurses termed "sundowning."

During brief times of confusion, I didn't know whether to pretend that I didn't know what Mom was talking about—giving her the added stress of explaining her thoughts—or to show by saying nothing that I understood all too well that she was confused, and thereby increase her anxiety. Whenever I couldn't decide, the uncertainty made me uncomfortable. Then all the training of my past kicked in, telling me this is where patience wins out over rushing into making a decision, when none needs to be made at the moment.

When Mom fell asleep, I left. After getting stuck at three traffic lights and one railroad crossing, I was home. Once inside my house, I lay down, hooked the heels of my boots on the armrest of the sofa, pried my boots off, and let them drop to the floor. That night I slept the entire night in my clothes, not waking once to even realize I wasn't in my bed.

Chapter 3

Three days later, I visited Mom again. She asked me a question as soon as she spotted me walking into her apartment. She was tired of needles, tired of getting her blood checked, tired of medications. She was tired of sitting in the same chair of the same apartment.

"Steve, can we go somewhere for a couple of hours?" she asked hopefully. "If a woman only lives in her memories, she's already dead. Let's do something fun. Let's go breathe some fresh air."

"Where do you want to go?" I asked.

"Let's go to Bohrer Park and sit under the trees. It looks like a nice day outside. Nurse Sylvia said you have approval to drive me, as long as we're back for my meds at dinner time. We have two or three hours to enjoy the nice weather outside."

The park was named in memory of George E. Bohrer, a county councilman, who served the sixth district in St. Louis in the late 1950's. Century-old maples and oaks, many of them despoiled to accommodate power lines, still grow in scatterings beyond the main entrance and parking lot. At the edge of the park, there is a strange little rock-bedded playground that will fill the shoes of any child or adult who dares enter. For miles in every direction, people drive over patched and re-surfaced county roads to visit the park from their neighborhoods.

As Mom made her suggestion, I felt joy and sadness run through me at the same instant. My thought of enjoying the nice weather with Mom was scrambled with the realization that I was at a loss to provide any long-term solution to her health problems. Both of us were hoping for a little temporary respite from the struggles that had galvanized our daily routines.

Within twenty minutes of signing out on the register at the front desk, Mom and I found a parking space close to the nearest unoccupied picnic table. It was a temperate, slightly overcast Saturday afternoon, with a breath of a breeze making the outdoors comfortable. It took me a few moments to wrestle Mom's wheelchair out of the backseat of my Dodge Ram pickup. In her apartment at Bethesda, Mom could get around using her walker for short distances, but when venturing out, she needed her wheelchair. Pushing the thing gave me the benefit of leaning and taking pressure off my sore back, without having to admit to anyone that maybe I was closer than I thought to needing a cane to walk myself. Once I had Mom in her wheelchair, I steered a course on a path that ran almost straight to the picnic table I had my sights on.

I walked slowly so as to not jar Mom. With one hand she held onto the armrest, while she tightly clutched her purse with the other. She insisted on bringing it even though it was lighter and contained fewer items than when she was healthier and more active. I looked down and saw Mom was smiling. The afternoon was allowing me another opportunity to be inspired by my sick mother, who could manage a few smiles, even though her elevated blood sugar and irregular heartbeat had a constant way of draining the natural color from her face. I hoped I could be so courageous when the time came for me to face my own last years on this earth.

"Let's take the picnic table by the pond over there under the big oak," said Mom. "If we go any farther into the woods, the trees will block our view."

"Okay. We'll have shade for maybe an hour, until the sun shifts farther west," I said, hoping to sit and relax once we were situated.

On the pond, we could see four ducklings riding on their mama's back between her folded wings, as the mother paddled across the pond's reedy edges. Ducks were the center of attention for the picnickers visiting this park on any given day. Rabbits poached in the high grasses just a stone's throw away from our position. The water in the pond was clear to the bottom except for a small section on the other side covered over by a velvet-green moss. We stopped, Mom sitting in her wheelchair and me on the near side of the picnic table, as squirrels shook limbs from tree to tree and dashed across the ground, then reversed the process to return to their original post to break open their findings. "See my silly-looking reflection in the water?"

asked Mom. "Don't I look awful ... When I'm gone, I hope you'll remember me for the person I was when I still had energy and a sharp mind."

"Your body is just the container, Mom," I answered. "What I love about you is what's always been inside. It doesn't change with time."

Mom smiled again at that. I laid down my jacket, my keys, and Mom's purse on the picnic table. About ten paces behind us, parks department workers had recently planted a row of shrubs as a windbreak. It was easy to tell the landscaping was new because the bushes were scrawny and too young to have needed any trimming yet. Clumps of sod and fresh piles of dirt were evidence against the workers trying to hide any of their recent efforts digging. If it had been me working on this project, before going home at the end of the day, I would have smoothed out the soil with the flat side of a shovel. The end of everything great, I thought, is when people start abandoning their pride and ambition, and replacing it with just enough effort to get by. Their work starts to look like flowers trying to survive underwatering, their beautiful blooms wilting and falling to the ground, instead of growing and reaching out to abundant rays of sunshine.

"I've been thinking," said Mom. She then made several curious choking sounds. "Shoot, now I forgot what I was going to say."

Mom never wore a mask. She was just confident enough to allow herself to be vulnerable and honest if something was working against her. I loved that about her.

"So Mom, does that mother duck and her ducklings remind you of raising your own four kids?"

"A mother duck is heroic in her own way. She has to endure thousands of little inconveniences and blows battering her world. She takes care of her young by herself, without the use of technology. I raised my children in a different time, before technology existed," said Mom.

"I must admit you did a pretty good job explaining to your kids the reasons for acting a certain way. Though we didn't always listen to you, we always knew you had our best interests in mind."

"I tried."

Bugs called water-skaters—poised like weightless statues on the surface of the pond—guaranteed the notice of park visitors during the day, but the tunes chirped by crickets were heard only by early morning joggers running along the trails of the park. The surroundings were plump with vegetation and critters, but much as she loved Nature, Mom craved only one kind of living thing when she was downhearted: a visit from her sister and a hug from one of her daughters or granddaughters.

"Looking at the water makes me wonder if we should move to a beach in California," I said. You could live close to your sister Rose." I jokingly added: "There would be less laundry to do, since we could wear bathing suits much of the day."

"Yeah, me in a bathing suit. That's a great idea," said Mom.

"You could find out if your bikini still fit," I said.

"When I was young and had the body to wear a bikini, I wore a one-piece bathing suit," said Mom. "We were more modest in those days."

"You have to admit that warm air drifting in from the ocean and the sweet smells of the sea would lift the mood in our souls," I said. "Aunt Rose can attest to the climate, culture, and beauty of California."

It was late in the afternoon, and we were both thirsty after having spent nearly two hours in the warm air and under partial sunlight. We were a few months short of the full summer bursting upon us with high and clear blue skies helping radiate the sun's intense heat. I turned toward Mom, still sitting in her wheelchair and under the dappled shade of the big oak. Seeing her feet bent at an uncomfortable angle, I propped her legs up on a Styrofoam cooler discarded by previous picnickers. With the sun now behind a large cloud, Mom pushed back the brim of her floppy fedora hat, making the deep shadow over the top half of her face disappear. I pulled out two water bottles, the ice inside them now mostly melted, from a storage pouch on the side of the wheelchair and handed one to Mom.

"I need to walk back to my truck and get something," I told her. I'll be back in a couple of minutes."

"Okay."

I walked to my truck, pushed the unlock button on my remote key, opened the driver's side door, and reached behind the seat for a paper bag holding a surprise. I scrunched and rolled both sides of the top of the bag with both hands to get a firmer grip.

After walking back to the spot under the oak, I set the paper bag down on the picnic table.

"I was going to wait until I was finished to show you this, but it's almost finished anyway, so open the bag to reveal your surprise."

"I remember the surprise you gave to the homeless man."

"What are you talking about?"

"I'm the old person here. You don't remember the homeless man at the bowling alley? A homeless man walked into the bowling alley to get out of the cold. You were in line to buy a hamburger and lemonade at the snack counter."

"I do remember watching you and Dad bowl one night. Dad had a perfect game going into the tenth frame, but he threw a split, and there went that."

"When it was your time to order, you told the lady behind the counter that the hamburger and lemonade was for the man with the grey beard, wearing old clothes, and sitting over by the side door of the bowling alley."

"I didn't know you were watching me."

"In passing and in a hurry to the ladies room, I saw what you did. I didn't say anything to you because I didn't want to miss my turn to bowl. And besides, it was pretty exciting with Dad having that perfect game going and everything. In retrospect, what you did was much more important than any perfect game in bowling. I should have told you then, but at least I'm telling you now."

"I do remember that night. I remember John Goodman, the actor, bowled in your league."

"That was before he became famous. He was the youngest bowler, and Dad and I were the oldest. Though I forgot to mention it, I was very proud of you that night. I knew I had raised you right."

"I guess that was a special night."

"So what is this special surprise you have for me today?"

"Open this bag I brought you, and find out."

Mom pulled my gift out of the bag. "Wow," she said. "What a beautiful photo album."

"All the pictures you had stuffed into a shoebox, I organized and stuck in there. The album was black leather and large enough to accommodate a large number of photos.

In 1935, Kodak was the first American company to introduce color film based on a special darkroom process to develop pictures. Red, blue, and green emulsions were used to process all the colors of the spectrum, but somehow this new product never caught on. The Polaroid Company introduced and mass-marketed instant color film in 1963. The whole world turned from grainy black-and-white to luminous full color overnight because a device in the form of a small box could sense color the same way the human eye does.

Over the years, before digital cameras were invented, our family members took turns taking pictures on holidays and special occasions. Rolls of film had to be dropped off for developing at the drugstore, and two or three days later, a family member returned to pick up the photos. After everyone in the immediate family had a chance to look at the new pictures, they were stuffed in a shoebox for safekeeping. Some photos were in black-and-white. After 1963, many of our family photos were taken using cameras with Polaroid's instant color film.

Looking through all the pictures of my three sisters playing with their Barbie dolls, blowing bubbles in the backyard, and playing with their hula hoops, one detail caught my attention. My sisters were almost always wearing something new or different in the photos, while I always had a nice pair of tennis shoes, called athletic running shoes today. Mom and Dad were usually wearing the same clothes on different holidays, more evidence of how much they sacrificed for their children.

In the shoebox, there were several pictures of my sisters playing hopscotch. Without the invention of computers, cell phones, video games, cable television, or the Internet yet, youngsters went outside and found things to do for entertainment. Hopscotch was the game my sisters played in the driveway and sometimes in the street in front of the house. This game has many variations around the world, but the version of the game played by my sisters, generally had nine squares, which together formed an oval pattern resembling an egg. And between "heaven" and "earth" was where all the action and all the competition of endless possibilities took place. One of my sisters would toss the marker, usually the piece of chalk, to one of the squares inside the oval. And from the starting point, "earth," participants carefully hopped on one leg through nine squares until they reached the end point, heaven, and then carefully hopped back to earth. We neighborhood boys participated once in a while, but usually we watched the girls have their fun.

"When we look at black-and-white photographs, we think the old days were gloomy times filled with grey scenery and dusty conditions," I said.

"There was just as much color then as there is today. Digital technology is just better at capturing all the colors now," said Mom.

"Here's a picture of me sitting on a corner stool after Dad ordered me to stay there and not leave my room. Kathy had told Dad I pushed her playing hopscotch, but I hadn't. Dad told me, 'Boys don't push girls,' and he locked me in my room. I guess Kathy figured if I was locked in my room, I couldn't bother her girlfriends when they came over to play," I said.

"Because you were the only boy, I worried that your father was too tough on you sometimes," said Mom.

"Here's a picture of Dad's 1980 Plymouth Fury, the car Patti swore she never wrecked, then twenty years later confessed to it. I was the number-one suspect for years."

"Your father suspected each of his children did it, and for a time, he even suspected his own wife wrecked the car and was afraid to tell him," said Mom.

"Here's a picture of George W. Bush. His staff sent you this signed photo after you mailed a contribution to the Republican Party. Did you hear the news about our governor?"

"Governor Nixon? No," said Mom.

"He just bought a new personal airplane that costs six-million dollars."

"I think the state should have purchased that old truck from the Beverly Hillbillies and let the governor travel around on the back roads in that," said Mom.

"That's funny," I said.

"A driver is cheaper than a pilot. An old truck is a lot less expensive than a new airplane."

"That's a little extreme, but I get your point. What does the governor do anyway?" I asked. "The only things we hear about are the campaign promises and the political fundraisers when he comes to town, wasting our time and money."

"They just keep finding more ways to spend taxpayers' money for their own agenda. The Roman Empire fell because the government extended well past its means. It's a good thing the Obama administration isn't doing that," said Mom. "I'm being facetious."

"I know you are," I said. "In effect no crime is committed when the work of a criminal is covered up by the media."

"When white-collar criminals, like cheating politicians, are caught with their hands in the cookie jar, they should be impeached and sent to prison just like street criminals who go to jail for committing crimes," said Mom.

She wasn't kidding, either. Mom believed modern politicians rush to send out their messages only to gain votes, instead of thoroughly studying issues to fix problems so the solutions make sense for the long run. Too much money is wasted on rushed programs like "Cash for Clunkers," "The Sea Monkey Project," "Keep the Kardashians on TV Project," and the "Why are Clowns Scary? Project," according to Mom.

"That's how I look at the whole mess," she said. "And our youth need to hear truthful words, not rhetoric that spreads false hope and flattering, unattainable promises," said Mom.

"This talk coming from the Democrats about healthcare is baloney," I said. "They tell us certain services will get added for free, and premiums will go down. Nothing is free. Someone will have to pay."

"My grandchildren will have to pay," said Mom.

"Here is a penciled sketch that one of your grandchildren must have drawn," I said.

"Allison is the artist in the family. I think she was in the third or fourth grade when she gave me that. I was still working as a nurse, and she wanted to surprise me with her interpretation of what a hospital looked like. The sketch of the front entrance and the building looks great, but I don't think many hospitals have a McDonalds, a Steak-n-Shake, and a Donut Shop attached to three sides of the main building."

"She has always had a vivid imagination," I said. "Come to think of it, Amanda sketches well too. I remember her drawing pictures of frogs, dogs, and other animals when she was in grade school."

"Shortly after your father and I bought our house, a traveling painter rang the doorbell and begged to be allowed to paint our portrait. Your father was very soft-hearted about anyone trying to sell things for a living, probably because he was in sales himself," said Mom. "Well, the painter set up his easel in our living room and did a portrait of your father and me. I was suffering from a seasonal heat rash on the side of my face, but nothing could persuade your father from changing his mind about the two of us staying in one position long enough for the painter to catch our likeness."

"Did the painter talk to you while he worked?"

"He was so full of it. He complimented his own work, saying to me his painting was such a true likeness, especially of you, Audrey. My dear, you have such an innocent look. I bet you never swear, and your dimples keep you from ever mouthing an angry thought."

"Do you remember saying anything back to the painter?" I asked.

"No, but I remember him dipping his brush, wiping some of the paint off the tip, and signing his illegible initials in the lower right-hand corner of the canvas. I was happy when he was finished."

"How'd the portrait look? I don't remember ever seeing it."

"That's because we never hung it on the wall. I looked like a chipmunk, partly because of my rash and swollen face, and partly because the painter's style was similar to that of a cartoonist," said Mom. "I doubt that painter ever became famous."

It was time to drive Mom back to Bethesda. We decided to stop at the grocery store to pick up a few snacks to put in the small fridge of her apartment. I pushed Mom in her wheelchair down several isles of the store. We bought three cups of Greek yogurt, a bag of oranges, a six-pack of Diet Coke, a pint of butter-pecan ice-cream, and a package of pre-sliced blueberry bagels. As we paid for these items in the checkout lane, a female clerk addressed me.

"Go ahead and push the green button on the credit card machine," she said. Distracted by her command after only signing my first name, I did.

"I think I'll start telling people to address me only as Steve, like Beyonce, Cher, Elvis, and other famous people," I said as we left the store.

Back in the car, and about a mile further down the road, Mom noticed a real estate sign that listed the agent's name as John John. Mom pointed it out. "Maybe someday you will be a famous author and be known as Steve Steve."

I grinned at her local joke, then asked, "Hey, Mom, you know how I like to read adventure books, right?"

"About as much as I like to read my mystery novels," said Mom.

"Well, I really enjoyed my last two books. One was about a woman's journey along the Pacific Crest Trail, the other was about a man's journey along the Appalachian Trail," I said. "I was thinking ..."

"It's good to think," said Mom.

"Stop, allow me to finish. I was thinking, since a blind man with a seeing-eye dog and a woman using a cane have already added their names to the Appalachian Trail record books, you and I could be the first mother-son duo to complete the feat using a wheelchair, me pushing you," I said.

"Well I'm certainly not going to push *you*," said Mom. "Are you crazy? After everything that has happened to me, do you think I want to die rolling off a cliff in a wheel chair?"

"You have to admit, it would be an ambitious feat. We would become household names."

"I already gave up on one household," said Mom, miserably.

"Sorry, Mom. It was my intention to end our conversation on a happier tone," I muttered.

It was after five by the time Mom and I returned to Bethesda. The temperature had dropped. When we got out of my truck, no precipitation was in evidence, but the low clouds and winds whipping around our heads were heavy with the smell of an approaching storm. Mom liked rain. There was something about that distinctive moisturizing fragrance that helped her heart beat regularly, no matter what else was going on around her.

It was time for Mom to take her meds and meet with one of the nurses who usually gave her insulin shots, either Nurse Sylvia or Nurse Iesha. Marveling at the peace and quiet, I watched as Sylvia administered the shot this evening. Mom sat in her chair and closed her eyes, ready to take a nap. I thought about how badly I needed a nap myself. I was one of the far-too-many working adults getting by on far too little sleep.

Often it's easy to spot when a person is tired. The intensity of their voice drops, they enunciate poorly, and there are pauses at long intervals for no obvious reason. Often a tired person is a caregiver for another person. Since Mom had come to Bethesda, my life had become a round of going to work, sleeping a few hours, and getting up early to visit Mom before it was time to go to work again. I was starting to feel the strain and knew I couldn't go on like this indefinitely.

Chapter 4

The aging of the baby boom generation, combined with the increase of average life expectancy, has produced the likelihood that a parent, due to suffering from illness or from a deliberating injury, will eventually need help from one of their middle-aged children. Medicare helps pay for some of the bills, but doesn't come close to adequately paying day-to-day expenses. Almost always one child or one friend steps up to help out. Adult children can choose to spend their money taking vacations or buying a bigger house or a fancier car. They can choose to help care for a sick parent or not. When the cost of a parent's needs is not shared by all siblings, the ones doing the work don't necessarily supply less care. But for the siblings providing the help, they are forced to reallocate time and money away from activities in ways that reduce their own consumption and leisure time. Of course, the welfare of a suffering parent is supposed to be part of a loved one's own standard of living.

Most individuals live much of their adult lives as either givers or takers. When a relative becomes seriously ill, it becomes clear which family members are which. Some individuals go out of their way to help comfort, while others go out of their way to avoid a difficult situation until the end, when there might be something to be gained by inheritance. Takers are the first people to complain about something that goes wrong or something they would have handled differently, when almost always they had never offered anything to help during the most unyielding times. When a sick person and a care partner only receive token support calls from other family and friends who then vanish, they must accept the strength that can be drawn from others who know how to share the pain of their grief, so that on their difficult path, they do not walk alone.

When an elderly person is upset about something or loses a loved one, people think their grief is minimized because older people have more experience and they are better equipped with skills for coping with tragedy. But the elderly need help with clinging to tightly to their sorrow. Grievers need to be reminded that their loved one lived, not only that they died. Or as a beautiful saying puts it, "Don't cry because it's over. Smile because it happened."

Mom had given me power of attorney for her financial affairs and her advanced health directive if needed someday. Having power of attorney is all about listening to others, so I invited my Aunt Rose from San Diego and my three sisters to meet me at the house where Mom raised her family—to weigh in, so to speak. Patti declined the invitation, but the other three ladies were pleased to accept.

Two days before Aunt Rose arrived in town, I cleaned my house, did my laundry, and shopped for extra supplies of paper products. I stocked my pantry with some extra food. There is a certain art to hosting relatives or friends at your home, but I never graduated to the level of host that gives their guests welcome kits including things like toothpaste, shampoo, conditioner, and soap. Because Aunt Rose packed smart, brought everything she needed, and always pitched in, she was a fun guest to have in the house. Neither she nor I acted like each other's servant.

My horoscope on the day of the meeting sent me a clear message. It read, "Stick to your guns. Don't change your mind, even if doing so will please someone else. Standing by your convictions will gain you far greater respect then knuckling under to pressure. Sympathy is the key to success this week." Whoever wrote this was unaware of the strength and stubbornness of the women in my family. Since my father died, my life had migrated toward something like the existence of a drifter in a world surrounded by pink. Kathy was living the life of a professional medical researcher, Karen refused to yield to anyone if she thought she was right, and Patti had developed a tough exterior from moving from city to city. My two daughters had become strong, independent women, and it was amazing how well Aunt Rose handled all of our weaknesses. Her assessments of us were straight and accurate, but not dangerous, because kindness was at the heart of them. She never talked behind people's backs.

Aunt Rose hardly looked seventy-nine, a surprise to any person hearing a comment about her age. Only her wisdom gave any hint of the number of her years on this earth. A little woman, with sturdy shoulders and one leg more swollen than the other due to a knee replacement, she lived her life with much energy. She had a perfect forehead, round face, dainty nose, and sculpted chin. She wore perfume that actually smelled good, not the teargas kind some women wear. Her fluffy brown hair was styled fashionably. Her dark eyes drew you into her fine face, with its frequently projected candid expressions. She possessed a heart of gold and a soul filled with goodness.

When I and all the females had all assembled, I presented my plan for their approval: the things remaining in the house that Mom did not want or need at her Bethesda apartment, would go to Goodwill.

"Oh no," my sisters said in unison, just as I had suspected.

"I want the china, as a reminder of all the good Sunday dinners," Kathy said.

"That belonged to our great-grandmother, on Mom's side," said Karen.

"Ah," I said.

"I know you saved some photos, but I want the old ones of Mom, when she was young," said Kathy. "Those pictures are part of our family history. I'll bet Patti would like some, too."

I paused and placed my hand on my heart. Life is simple and complicated at the same time. Apparently what a son thinks has value is not what the females of a family see as valuable. I had no idea they'd care about the dishes. This was just the beginning, and the day was going to involve a lot of sorting out.

I felt tired, not at all in the mood to facilitate the discussions and debates I saw on the agenda for the rest of the afternoon. When a parent is under someone else's care, time takes on a whole new meaning. For me on most days of the week, when it turned dark, I went to work. When the morning rush hour traffic stirred, I got up, readied myself, and drove to Bethesda to spend a couple of hours visiting with Mom. Everything between work and Bethesda was mostly about fitting in sleep, grabbing a bite to eat, and paying attention to the important details requested of me. At least that is what I did before Aunt Rose came to town. She and I would soon start alternating shifts with my sisters. On the days I didn't get enough sleep the night before, I walked around like a zombie in Zen mode. Because my judgments and intuition were compromised at those times, I started planning regular naps, usually three hours before the sun rose and two hours in late afternoon. This was working for me. When I got enough sleep, my existence improved to that of a semi-intelligent zombie, one with more awareness and an awakened brain.

"You all have to take what you want then," I said, looking directly at my sisters. "You know what organizing consultants say, 'If you haven't used it in two years, throw it away,'" said Karen.

Her comment scared me a little bit. What would Dad

do? What would Mom want? I decided to take a step back and try to relax a little, just letting the day play out.

The old playroom in the basement, still in good shape and framed in sheets of four-by-eight walnut paneling, suffered from an overcrowding of stored items. Kathy and Karen's old Barbie dolls were stored in two torn and tattered plastic cases, one red and the other blue. In a cardboard box were a few dozen Barbie outfits—tiny dresses, hats, purses, and shoes that no one had touched in thirty years. A broken record player, a pile of outdated garments, and a stack of board games—including Candy Land, Monopoly, Yahtzee, Mouse Trap, Battleship, and the Game of Life— occupied an entire corner section of the playroom. Against the wall, on the opposite side, sat a vintage century-old Singer sewing machine and table.

Borrowing Kathy's i-phone, I typed the words "vintage Singer sewing machine" into the search bar to find out more information. One resulting web match was the home page of the Singer Sewing Company, but the site was under renovation. Eventually my research revealed that because the factory had made nearly a quarter-million of theses machines every year after 1900, our family heir-loom was less precious and unique than I had assumed. Singer began manufacturing sewing machines in 1851 at a factory in Clydebank, England, not far from Glasgow. In the beginning, their machines were so expensive that the company had to implement a payment plan for their cus-tomers. Eventually market demand and refined production methods made the purchase of sewing machines more affordable for the average family. World-famous for a long time, Singer was the biggest sewing machine factory on the globe when it was bombed heavily during WWII. The factory tried to hang on for parts of four decades in Glasgow, but the original headquarters was finally closed and demolished in the 1980s. The train station is still there and the housing complex that now stands on the land of the old manufacturing site is named "Singer." Sometimes the value of things is more about sentiment than money. The Singer sewing machine that was passed down in our family, it turns out, is more valuable as a story than valuable to a collector.

On the unfinished side of the basement was a small table covered in paint cans, brushes, rags, and a set of small screwdrivers in a clear-plastic case. Underneath a window and resting on the concrete floor was another old sewing machine with a box of spare parts next to it. On the top of a workbench was a small toolbox with a hammer, two kinds of pliers, a measuring tape, and a crescent wrench. A coffee can filled with galvanized roofing nails sat next to the toolbox. A spool of wire, a metal hacksaw, and a set of tire chains hung on hooks inserted in the floor joists overhead. In a large basket was a pile of soiled clothes and an old pair of size-ten pigment-stained tennis shoes Dad wore when he was working in the yard or painting the house.

On a shelf above the washing machine, a black-and-white picture of my father's never-married great-great-aunt, who worked as a seamstress, dominated the space.

Her face, her wrinkles, the certain exhaustion in her eyes made me think she was about eighty-five at the time the photo was taken. This put the year of her birth around 1860, President Abraham Lincoln's election year. More than likely, when she was a young woman, she rode a horse or sat in a buggy to get places.

In another shoebox, my sisters found early photos of people none of us recognized. I was sure some of them were of Mom's Irish ancestors. Though it was unlikely I would ever identify any of the people in the pictures, throwing them away seemed like a betrayal of the courage they exhibited to get here. So even without a designated purpose for the photographs, I took the shoebox out of the basement to store in a safe place in the basement at my house.

Next thing I knew, I was prying open boxes we hadn't looked inside for thirty years. Bringing home stuff to put in my garage might help create a nice warehouse appeal, but I was against crowding a place with already limited space. Restraint was called for.

When I pulled out a fancy wooden box filled with silver cutlery, I was surprised to find that neither sister showed much interest. I knew Mom wanted this passed down after she was gone. There were five silver knifes, fifteen silver forks of different shapes and sizes, a scooped silver spoon for serving stew or soup from a pot, five silver spoons, and a very old corkscrew with a silver handle. Each tarnished item bore the same crest design, each piece being part of a set. Velvet-lined grooves inside the box protected each item.

"Karen, you are the perfect person to inherit the set of silverware," said Aunt Rose, knowing how much Karen liked to cook.

"Yes, Karen," I put in, "especially since you've once collected silver spoons as a hobby. This set will just add to your collection."

Karen wheeled around. "I don't appreciate you all telling me what I should take home with me."

"We just thought you might like them," said Aunt Rose.

"No, you're trying to spoon-feed me Mom's tastes, which are different than mine," Karen protested.

"But this is *silver*-spoon-feeding," Kathy muttered.

At that, Karen laughed. She laughed so hard she had to sit down on the floor.

"Sorry. I should take them. I guess I'll have to start cooking more fancy meals. No more TV dinners for Mike and me."

"So I'll take the china," said Kathy. "It's already neatly boxed. All you'll have to do for me, Steve, is take the two boxes to a UPS or FedEx outlet. You wouldn't mind, would you?"

"I'll take a few boxes of clothes to sell at our neighborhood garage sale next month," said Karen. "I'm sorry if we're changing all the plans you had for cleaning out Mom's house, but you have to admit, you did call us for help. If we make any money, I'll give it to you to put in Mom's checking account."

Nearly thirty boxes of clothes and miscellaneous things were hauled to Karen's house for the garage sale. She made about two-hundred dollars, and the money went into Mom's checking account.

"I'm getting hungry," Kathy said after we'd worked for a while. I could go for a good meal right now of fish and chips."

"I remember when chips meant a bag of wood bits used to start a fire in a barbecue pit, and hardware was something you bought to fix appliances," I said.

"Pot was something you cooked in, and coke was a cold drink," said Aunt Rose.

While I'm not sure if Aunt Rose ever gave much thought to having been the youngest of three girls, I wondered if that explained her relentless yearning for old family stories and appreciation of all things old. Probably not, because I was the oldest of four children, and I was the same way.

We all agreed it was time for a break, so I drove the bunch to a local restaurant that served fish and chips. The morning had stirred up many memories of days gone by. After lunch, over coffee, we sat around and reminisced.

"Your mother and I were best friends, like sisters, all our lives," Aunt Rose began.

"You are sisters. That's why we call you our aunt," said Kathy.

Aunt Rose winked and smiled. The truth was, next to her mama and papa and her two husbands that had died in other eras, Aunt Rose loved her sister Audrey more than anyone in the world. And of course, our dad and

Aunt Rose's two husbands had been good friends too.

"We did everything together. After each of us married and moved out of your grandparents' house, we lived with our husbands across the hall from each other in an apartment building in the city. We went to dances and movies, sang songs, and raised our children together." Aunt Rose's voice trailed off, and her head swayed slightly, as if she was remembering the sound of old music. "We shared everything, good times and bad. We were with each other at every one of our children's births."

"We have to keep our wonderful memories," said Kathy.

"When times are good and everything is comfortably in order, it is easy to become contented," said Aunt Rose. "Troubled times teach us lessons that last for the rest of our lives."

"I hesitate to go as far and say that troubled times are necessary evils, but they do eventually end, and we push forward," I said. "We do gain strength by using our resources and skills to search for solutions and help our family members and friends."

Aunt Rose said that after I was born, nearly every married woman living in the housing flats and apartment buildings nearby started having babies. I'd like to think that because they saw me as such a special child, they wanted a baby of their own. Of course the baby boom had nothing to do with me. The economy was good, interest rates were low, America was still in a rebuilding mode after two big wars, interstates were connecting cities, and men could pick and choose where they wanted to work. Mothers stayed home to raise their children because their husband's paycheck, with some occasional overtime pay, was usually enough to pay the bills for the family. But during the first few years of their marriage, it was a hardship for my parents to make their monthly house payments and pay all the other expenses, despite the wages my father earned. My parents could barely feed themselves, much less the additional mouths of me and my sister Kathy. Mom served lots of bologna and peanut butter sandwiches to save money on groceries, and she lowered the thermostat a few degrees during cold weather to save on energy costs to heat the house. Dad drove a used car and always paid cash for purchases he deemed as bare necessities, trying his best to give every member of the family what they needed. I hesitated to ask for too many things, because even as a young boy, I realized how hard my parents worked just to get by. I figured any added pressure directed at my father only meant longer work hours when he would be away from me. I was unaware of it then, but plenty of ten- and twelve-hour working days would fill my life later, just like they did at that time for my father.

One of my earliest recollections of my parents was watching the two of them dance together to the music of Herb Alpert and the Tijuana Brass on the living room record player.

"Aunt Rose, do you remember Herb Alpert and the Tijuana Brass?" I asked.

"Of course, my sisters and I listened to that band all the time," she replied.

"When I was a little boy, an album cover of the band sat on the coffee table at our house," I said. "That album spun on the record player every weekend."

"Which album was it?"

"From what I recall, they released an album or two each year throughout the 1960s," I said. "The one Mom and Dad liked was called, "Whipped Cream," and I think it sold something like six- or seven-million copies in the United States."

"I remember it. That cover featured actress/model Dolores Erickson wearing only what appeared to be whipped cream," said Aunt Rose.

"It wasn't really whipped cream?"

"Real whipped cream would have melted under the heat of studio lights. In reality, she was wearing a white blanket covered in massive amounts of shaving cream."

"I doubt many men ever found out about that illusion," I said.

"Did you know Herb Alpert played the part of the drummer on Mt. Sinai in the film, "The Ten Commandments"?" asked Aunt Rose.

"No, but I remember watching the band when they appeared on TV variety specials. Their performances gave a visual interpretation of the music from their latest album. Herb Alpert made music videos before MTV even existed," I said.

"No one in Alpert's band was actually Hispanic either.

Alpert used to say his group consisted of four lasagnas, two bagels, and one slice of American cheese," Aunt Rose said with a chuckle. "The band's success spawned other Mexican acts, like the Baja Marimba Band. Mexican ties to the U. S. are more common today, with the culture of dance and cuisine from south of the border available just around the corner in every American city. I wonder if Herb Alpert's music had something to do with that?"

After lunch, the ladies and I returned to the house to finish our project. Going through one box of old stuff, I marveled at some of the things Mom had saved ... souvenirs from the Arch, the St. Louis Zoo, the Fox Theatre, Grant's Farm, the Missouri Botanical Garden, the St. Louis City Library, and the Missouri History Museum. Mom loved her hometown. She loved living in St. Louis and rooting for the Cardinals baseball team. Outsiders might think St. Louis lacks greatness, but the outdoor fun and the urban buildings you can get lost in here, are proof it is a special city. I remember Mom saying, "St. Louis has everything. And if that's not enough, we have good interstates to take drivers to some of the best hospitals in the country. Oh yeah, and some fun casinos too." St. Louis grocers import Iowa corn and New York bagels, and if you would rather eat out, there are some terrific Italian and family-style restaurants in town. The metropolitan area is an anomaly with the hospitality of a small town and the commercial appeal of a big city. St. Louis was built by the hard work and ingenuity of its founders. Almost all of the early immigrants to St. Louis came to America to escape from tyranny in their home country and to live in freedom.

One liberty that the citizens of St. Louis treasure is going to Cardinals baseball games, spending their entertainment dollars and escaping the stresses of everyday life. This time of year, the outfield grass at Busch Stadium, freshly mowed in a crisscross pattern, looks like a checkerboard in two shades of green.

We all agreed to dedicate two boxes of slightly used shoes to Karen's next garage sale. She had discovered after her first garage sale that comfortable, like-new shoes are in demand almost everywhere. Another box of junk, mostly broken items, we set at the curb for the next trash pickup. Several other boxes we designated for Goodwill. Neither my sisters nor I broke out in hives at the thought of giving away some items still considered useable. I was happy knowing I was raised in a family that tried to give a little back.

I was happy with how our project was going, everyone getting along and agreeing on what ought to go where. "See, this is what happens when the person with power representing the family knows how to take charge," I said.

"Just listen to him," said Kathy. "We all know it's the women-folk running the show here," said Karen, and we all had a laugh.

"What's in all these other boxes?" asked Aunt Rose, looking over the rim of her glasses.

"More clutter, probably," said Karen.

"These boxes aren't clutter," said Aunt Rose. "They are your Mom's life."

"If you see anything you can use, please take it," I said.

Once we opened the next few boxes, I was a little embarrassed I had offered them to Aunt Rose. We placed three more boxes of junk, which included a broken electric can opener, a worn-out toaster with a frayed power cord, and a turkey fryer too old and dangerous-looking to keep, at the curb for the next trash pickup. We filled two boxes with a set of unused glass mixing bowls, two sets of dinner plates, a mixture of mismatched eating utensils, and a few other small kitchen utensils that were in good shape.

"So, I guess you're not interested in having that old turkey fryer shipped back to San Diego?" I asked Aunt Rose.

"Even if I was, I think shipping it to San Diego would cost more than it is worth."

I loaded the good stuff into the back seat of my truck, then the ladies rode with me to the closest Goodwill Collection Center to drop off our donation.

"It's so great having you in town again," Kathy said to Aunt Rose, turning around in the front seat so she could face our elderly relative who sat with Karen in the back. "Tell us some more stories about Mom. What was she like in her early twenties? Did she have boyfriends?"

"There was another guy before your dad. His name was Wally, and your mother dated him for almost a year," Aunt Rose answered.

"What was he like?" Karen asked.

"His love for collecting snakes got her thinking

differently about him. He kept on getting snakes and adding them to aquariums throughout his house. He had dozens of them. Creepy," said Aunt Rose.

"Did Mom like him?" I asked.

"Wally was a good guy, but he was a little strange. Your mother told me she started having dreams where Wally appeared as a snake."

"Maybe when you're around snakes so much, you start slithering along just like they do," I said.

"Maybe," said Aunt Rose. "There were a lot of men who pursued your mom. She was an attractive woman," said Aunt Rose.

"What else sticks in your memory about those early years before Mom got married?" Kathy asked.

"Your mother loved to read books. It may seem odd, but even as a young newlywed, she spent time at the library searching for another book before she finished the one she was reading," said Aunt Rose.

"Reading. Oh, yes," I said. "We kids were the victims or the beneficiary of Mom's passion for reading, depending on how you look at it. She was always telling us to read books and stay up on current events because that was the best way to boost our intelligence." It's hard for me to remember the day I finally decided my mother was right, but somewhere during the dozens of times she told me that studying history and reading books and newspapers was important to increase a person's knowledge, I started reading everything I could get my hands on, for my own sake.

During her entire life, Mom read a wide range of genres, including politics, mysteries, pop culture, and social sciences. She also read each day to her young children, a habit that inspired us to become avid readers ourselves. Mom believed reading was an important ingredient of both success and happiness, and that a person who enjoys reading would never be truly lonely. They could always lose themselves in the world of a wonderful book.

"As young girls, your mother and I heard stories about the achievements of our great-grandfather. Some of them were overinflated, I'm sure," said Aunt Rose.

"Mom mentioned a few times that we had an ancestor from the Juengst side of the family who was an inventor," said Karen. "Is that who you mean?"

"Yes, that's him," said Aunt Rose. "He was my great-grandfather and your great-great-grandfather, and he fought on the Union side in the Civil War. Back in the mid 1800's, inventors and scientists were focused on finding things that could make living and staying alive a little easier."

"He helped invent axle grease or something," I said.

"That's right. He was part of a team that worked for George Washington Carver."

"I know George Washington Carver was born in Missouri," I said.

"If you think back to your high school studies, you may recall that Carver escaped much of the hardships of slavery because of his intellect. He became famous for discovering nearly three-hundred uses for peanuts," said Aunt Rose.

Kathy opened her laptop and googled Carver's name. "Listen to this," she said. "Carver worked on developing adhesive glue, metal polish, axle grease, fuel briquettes, synthetic rubber, ink, and wood stain to help Southern farmers. He also discovered over a hundred new ways to use soybeans, pecans, and sweet potatoes." The article said Carver was even more concerned with his students' character than with their intellectual development. He compiled a list of eight character traits for his team members to strive toward:

1) Live a clean life both inside and outside of work.
2) Live without looking up to the rich or looking down on the poor.
3) Lose, if need be, without squealing.
4) Win without bragging.
5) Always be considerate of women, children, and the elderly.
6) Be too brave to lie.
7) Be too generous to cheat.
8) Take your share of the world, and let others take theirs.

"He was a devout religious man," Aunt Rose said. "He wanted to destroy racial disharmony way before anyone ever heard about the Civil Rights movement."

"It sounds like George Washington Carver and my great-great-grandfather were amazing men," I said. I loved listening to Aunt Rose talk. She knew a lot about history and remembered so much about the past and the history of our family. When she got on a topic she was passionate about, which was often, she sounded a lot like Mom.

That evening after the girls went home, Aunt Rose and I came back to my place. We were exhausted from the day's work, but had just enough energy left to help each other put together a simple supper of salad and turkey sandwiches.

"Do you still go to Cardinals games?" asked Aunt Rose, chopping up fresh lettuce.

"Every chance I get," I said. "I should take you while you're here. Maybe we could even pack Mom up and take her with us."

"I'm pretty sure the wheelchair couldn't navigate the stadium stands," Aunt Rose answered, "but I'd love to go with you sometime. I'm still a Cardinals fan, you know, even if I do live in San Diego."

"It's the Padres' loss," I said.

"I watched a show on TV the other day, and the broadcaster said baseball is still first in the hearts of elderly sports fans," said Aunt Rose.

"The great thing about baseball is that every spring there is a new start with new hopes for a championship season. I think old purists enjoy the rhythm of the passing innings because baseball lets fans take advantage of the only modern team game without a clock," I said.

"It's only natural that older people love a sport where announcers never have to talk about how much time is left on the clock." I chuckled at that one. "I catch most of the games on television," I said. "One nice thing about watching baseball on TV is that each half-inning allows for a trip to the bathroom or a visit to the refrigerator."

"Baseball speaks to the soul of Americans. Each game is a marvelous story of overcoming obstacles, which is what matters most to people who are getting old," said Aunt Rose.

Chapter 5

Mom had been ill for nearly eight years, fighting diabetes, heart disease, and cancer. The loss of her husband had also taken its toll. Now, at the age of eighty-two, a large part of her income was spent on heart medications, cancer drugs, insulin shots, pain relievers, medical supplies, creams, and ointments. She slept a great deal; twelve hours a night was usual now. When she was healthier and ten years younger, she played golf and loved walking at the mall, though she never spent much money shopping other than for essentials. Now, other than doing her rehab exercises, she had little interest in physical activities. Walking up steps, over curbs, and around furniture was becoming more challenging.

Mom's life was unfolding faster than she wanted, so she tried to pace things in a variety of ways, taking her time and carefully thinking about the necessary steps to do even the simplest of physical tasks. She counted her steps when she walked, read signs out loud, and sang tunes when something reminded her of a happy occasion from the past.

The way the elderly residents walked told you whether their spirits were low or high. If a resident walked down the hall slowly, clearing his throat again and again, making thick phlegm sounds, not caring if it annoyed others, it probably was a bad day. In passing, if a resident flicked a hello at the air instead of at the person, it was probably a bad day. If a resident made an effort to walk to the dining room, then ignored all the food served at the table, it was probably a bad day. When I noticed ladies elevating their voices as they walked, wanting to be heard by others in conversation, it probably was a good day. For the hardcore elderly baseball fans, who walked to the recreation room to watch the Cardinals game together, seeing a player make a fantastic defensive play to end an inning, it was probably a good day. When the player who led off hit a home run winning the game, it was a great day.

Now, from the moment Mom woke in the morning at Bethesda, she was stuck and jostled and bothered. Every person trained in a different capacity who could get near enough wanted to grasp her hands or study her symptoms, all with good intentions. She had no private life anymore. Clothes that went for laundering by Karen came back much later than when she did the work herself. Table napkins and condiments were fought over at lunch and dinner. She could not go for a long walk, drive to a bank, or pop into a drugstore by herself like she could before. If she tried to use the bathroom, people followed, worried that she might fall. There was no place to cash a check. No part of her life was normal anymore, at least the way she was accustomed to doing things, and there was no prospect that it ever would be again. It was now harder for her, a woman used to living independently and having fun, to hide and avoid any extra attention.

I remember one particular morning vividly. Mom leaned toward the mirror to inspect her image. It was if she were looking at herself in a painting again. "Three times a day," she said, "I'm administered combinations of insulin, Coumadin, Digoxin, Klorcon, Atorvastatin, Ondansetron, Carvedilol, Torsemide, and Warfarin. I'm not sure all this is worth fighting anymore." It was amazing. We all know insulin is used by people with diabetes, but for her to recall the names of all the other eight medications she was taking floored me. Mom felt the years creep up on her like someone watching a mile-wide twister sweep across land in tornado alley at the height of storm season, but she still understood why she took certain medications. I was astounded. There is an arsenal of maturity, of old age, that requires toughness and technique that few young people respect or understand. Before her physical beauty and mental alertness started to crumble, leaving her sick, scarred, and feeling ridiculous, her life was full of excitement and success. Mom was famous for never giving up. But now she was allowing her mouth to droop as it wanted to, her eyelids to fall half-mast, and her thoughts to wander aimlessly. Before her in the mirror, she saw eighty-two years weighing her down, and whispers of the unknown were becoming overwhelming. But through it all, she managed to hold her shoulders square, not complaining that she needed a walker or a wheelchair to go anywhere. "I miss my old house, but I know it was too much work for me now. The old place is the only home I've known since your father and I signed the mortgage papers in 1956," said Mom.

"I know you worked hard to keep your marriage strong and our family happy together under one roof," I said.

"In the old days, a woman had to learn the art of giving, loving, serving, and praising, to keep a marriage strong. If she took out more than she put in, her marriage leaked out until it was empty."

"Things are different today," I said.

"A woman still has to know when to be bold enough to use her voice and brave enough to follow her heart," said Mom.

In walked Nurse Sylvia. She was making her afternoon rounds. "Hi, Audrey. How is my old friend today?" asked Sylvia.

"I seem to have a habit of collecting life-threatening illnesses," said Mom.

"There's that sense of humor again," said Sylvia.

"Hopefully it will lighten your mood, in case you are experiencing any problems today," said Mom.

"Sylvia, I can leave the apartment for a little while, so you can do your thing," I said.

"Don't be silly. I'm just going to give your mother her meds. She's doing a good job of making new friends here, by the way, aren't you, Audrey? Everybody here loves your mom."

"I put my head down and try to act like a good patient," said Mom.

"Mom, you don't need to act at all. Just give it some time to get acquainted with the staff and the other residents," I said.

"When I meet new people, I try to remember their names by associating some distinguishing feature with each person," said Sylvia, "like beautiful hair, pretty eyes, or a nice smile."

"Or ears that stick out, bruised hands, breathes through mouth, looks ill, walks with a limp, or one foot in the grave," said Mom.

"Audrey, you are so funny," said Sylvia with a laugh.

Maybe by joking with the doctors, the nurses, and me, Mom was able to laugh on the inside, otherwise we would have noticed a lot more crying on the outside. This is the way we would remember her once she was gone, a woman of substance who dealt with life squarely, facing whatever it had to hand her. And we would always remember the sacrifices she made, and how her family always took precedence. She loved her children and grandchildren. She loved the times she had cooked meals and served them to the family sitting around the dinner table. She believed that a lot of family problems could be eradicated if families just sat down at the dinner table together. Mom often told us as children, "The difference between ordinary and extraordinary is the little word extra, as in extra effort."

The wind was whipping around and rain started falling. With the sun-downing effect taking hold on Mom, I decided to drive back home before a full evening of rough weather settled over the city. While the residents at Bethesda were pretty inactive during the evening hours, almost always preferring to call it an early night, rabbits outside Mom's apartment window were scurrying in the remaining glimmers of light, and the birds were nestling into the bushes to avoid the bad weather approaching. Every ride home from the facility in my truck was different. Memories filled my head. Faces appeared and disappeared like clouds forming shapes, and scenes rose and faded on this ride home. I thought about broken promises, lies, kisses, weddings, funerals, a football game in the snow, a ketchup stain on a white shirt, a mother singing in the kitchen as she prepared a meal, and that all-of-a-sudden a moment when a daughter or son appears all-grown-up.

When tired enough, I can sleep for hours, but sometimes at dawn, in the minutes it takes for the sun to fully rise above the horizon, I blink awake like someone has turned on a switch. Sun gushes in through the window shades and pries open my eyelids.

Early the next morning, I decided to drive over to Mom's old house by myself. There was still loads to do, and I enjoyed the comfort of stepping into that old place which inside still looked as if no time had passed since I was a boy. When an elderly widow leaves her house and moves to an assisted living community, someone else has to clear out the belongings. Few elderly people migrate from paper to paperless without friction. Most hold on to everything bound to disappear from the world they knew before, such as: stationary, 35mm film, old tools, clothes lines, wash tubs, clip-on jewelry, typewriters, and old carpeting. Everything in Mom's house was old, and few things had been upgraded in thirty years. The furnace, water heater, air-conditioner, stove, refrigerator, garbage disposal, washer, dryer, toilet, shower, and faucets worked, but they were all old.

Cleaning out a house is a fool's errand, haplessly carrying around heavy objects, digging in the trash, looking for important papers, filling boxes, paying off the bills, organizing medical records. The job is full of distractions, and you're constantly unearthing things from the past that you want to examine and read, not because you need to for the clean-out but because of the memories they bring back and insights into the past that they provide. This morning I was rewarded with a gem of a discovery—an old letter from my father to my mother. He had read it to her, out loud in front of a crowd, on the occasion of their fiftieth wedding anniversary. I decided I would frame it and present it to Mom.

After spending five hours cleaning out parts of the house, I drove to Bethesda. Inside Mom's beautifully decorated apartment, the late afternoon sun slanted down through the shaded east window and fell across the tan textured carpet, the green wool La-z-boy, the dark-brown sofa, the new digital flat-screen TV, and the sliding-door closet built into the far wall. White ruffled curtains framed the sides of the window and a single green-and-white marble lamp stood on an end table in the corner. Visitors of other residents could be heard milling about in the early evening hour, about fifteen minutes before dinner was to be served by the seven-person kitchen staff. Riding over the quiet hubbub were the loud voices of the two young ladies at the sign-in desk in the lobby, relaying messages to visitors and staff via the public-address system.

After dinner, I decided to stay that evening and play Bingo with Mom and some of the residents, mostly women, in the activities building. I sat between Mom and Jim, the only other man playing Bingo that evening. Jim was a tall, thin man who dressed sharp and wore a suit and tie on Sundays. He had a little trouble concentrating enough to play more than one card, so I helped him cover numbers on a second card. Each of the ladies played three or four cards. Early on, because I was talking to Mom and not paying attention to the activities director calling the numbers, Jim caught me when I missed covering a number. He then playfully scooted both cards a few inches in his direction. When Mom and I later won three games in a row toward the middle of the session, he scooted both cards back over toward me. This made for a chuckle and broke the ice for more conversation.

"Where are you from, Jim?" I asked.

"I was born in St. Louis in 1924," he replied.

"Are you a Cardinals fan?"

"I watch every game on TV."

"I remember the entire starting lineup of the team that played in the World Series when I was ten years old," I said.

"When I was ten years old, the Gas House Gang played in the World Series," said Jim.

"I heard that team fielded some players with very shabby appearances," I said.

"Some of them looked shabby, but that team was tough," said Jim. "Five players who batted over .300 in the regular season."

"Do you remember the names of the team?" I asked.

"They had cartoonish nicknames. I remember those: Dizzy, Daffy, Ripper, Ducky, Buster, Pepper, Kiddo, Leo the Lip, Wild Bill, and The Fordham Flash," said Jim.

"I remember hearing about Dizzy Dean," I said.

"Ah, yes. Dizzy Dean. He once asked a batter he was facing, 'Son, what kind of pitch would you like to miss?' He was a character."

"I guess you would say he had plenty of confidence," I said.

"One time Dizzy Dean got hit in the head by a ball, and they had to do an x-ray. Afterward he said, 'The doctors x-rayed my head and found nothing. The Lord was good to me, because he gave me a strong body, a good right arm, and a weak mind.' Dizzy Dean had recurring headaches after that accident," said Jim, "but he never stopped being a character."

Jim was scraggly and salty and old-school. I liked him. He brought an edge to conversation, the kind that is cool and never goes out of style.

"That's pretty good," I said. "You have a good memory."

It was true that the elderly are able to remember things

from long ago, often better than they remembered things that happened yesterday or last week. Maybe it has something to do with happier times. Maybe it has something to do with stories they've told over and over.

"Don't ask me what I had for dinner last night," said Jim. "It's short-term memory that's hard for old people. I do pretty well with things from a long time ago, especially things I loved, like baseball."

"Were you ever married?" I asked.

"My wife died several years ago. When she was still alive, we lived in Peoria," he said. "When my health went downhill, a social worker recommended this place to me. My wife and I never had kids, and there's no family, so I rarely get visitors."

"I'm sure you miss your wife very much. I hope there is peace in your life, until the day the two of you are together again," I said.

"On Saturday afternoons, my wife and I would walk to the grocery store a few blocks from our house. During our last year together, I remember we were standing at an intersection one time, trying to catch our breath and each of us holding a bag of groceries, when neither of us could figure out which direction we needed to walk to get home. We stopped walking to the grocery store after that," said Jim, as he winked and slapped my back, letting out a trace of laughter.

"Sorry to hear that Jim," I said.

"If we only had to walk straight ahead, we wouldn't need any luck in life," he said.

"Good luck is nice, but peculiar and unexpected things make life interesting too. What's the strangest thing that happens to a man who's growing old?" I asked.

"Besides all the aches and pains, losing the hair on my head never bothered me. But it's amazing how well a man's eyebrows, the hair in his ears, and the hair in his nose grows when he gets old. I need to trim the hair in these places more often than when I had a full head of hair and went to the barber for a crew cut every week," said Jim.

"I'm starting to pay more attention to those areas when I shave now, too," I said.

After the last Bingo game was called, Jim reached into his pocket and pulled out a coin from a zipped inner pouch in his wallet.

"Here, this is my lucky nickel. I want you to have it. I've carried it in my wallet all my life," he said. "It will remind you to stay optimistic when you face more of those crossroads along the way."

I had compunction about taking Jim's lucky nickel. After spending just one evening with me, he wanted me— of all the people in the world—to possess his long-held keepsake. His pleasure in offering me his lucky nickel was so acute that you would have thought I had won some major victory. Perhaps I had. When you win something big, you know it right away, and it stays with you the next day, and all the days after. I'd sat in that Bingo hall only once, but part of me would never stop sitting there. A part of me was going to sit there for the rest of my life. Soap and water could never wash away, and my mind would never wish away, my memories of that evening.

"Oh, Jim, I can't take that," I said.

"I insist. I don't have a big family. You seem like a nice young man. I want you to have my lucky nickel," said Jim. "I carried it around with me, never sure when the mood would strike me to re-circulate it. Once I thought I lost it after leaving my wallet in a hotel room in Chicago. But an honest maid found the wallet in between an arm rest and seat cushion. She gave it to the night manager, and he shipped the thing to the address on my driver's license. The money and credit cards were all still there. The lucky nickel was still in the pouch."

Here was this elderly gentleman I just met, calling me a young man and insisting I take his lucky nickel. I would turn sixty-years-old in a few months, but I guess I was a young man to Jim at eighty-nine. I took the lucky nickel, shook Jim's hand, and thanked him.

"Tonight was a delight, a nice surprise," said Mom as we walked back to her apartment. "Are you hooked on Bingo now?"

"Maybe," I said. "I certainly enjoyed the conversation,"

I hugged Mom, said goodbye, and drove home. The next morning I awoke after a good night's sleep. I liked the first hour of the day and took pleasure in sipping hot coffee, checking emails, and catching on up local and national news.

Remembering something, I set down my coffee and

phoned Mom. "Last night, did I leave my black jacket on your sofa?" I asked.

"You did, and it's still lying there," she said. "Jim is still lying there, too, in his bed."

"What do you mean, Mom?"

"The coroner and the men from the funeral home haven't been here yet to pick up his body. Jim died in his sleep last night."

I was stunned. "I'm very sorry to here that," I said. I found myself getting choked up.

"Say an extra prayer for him when you go to sleep tonight," said Mom.

"I will."

"You never know around here when you might be talking to someone for the last time."

"Well, try not to worry about things," I said.

"I'll be okay," said Mom.

I knew Jim was going to a better place, an afterlife where everything is unknown until you get there. He was traveling to a wider world, embarked on a new adventure. But I was going to miss him. In just one meeting, he had given me so much. Facts of history, wonderful anecdotes, a glimpse into his life, and above all an item so precious and personal to him, his lucky nickel. And he had done all that on the last evening of his life. I would treasure that nickel forever.

A friendship is seldom gained instantly. It usually takes time to root itself. It needs a background of funny, wearisome, or even tragic events to link two people together. Sharing a book, a movie, or a meal can start a discussion and an experience with another person. Friendship is more than a sudden glimpse or acquaintance; it develops when two people are able to talk with confidence even at midnight, knowing there is trust surrounding their conversation. I hadn't had time to develop a full-blown friendship with Jim, but I like to think one would have developed over time. The rest of the day, I thought of Jim often, and said little prayers for him. I felt grateful knowing Mom was still there, always just a few miles away, anytime I needed her or anytime she needed me. And I knew she wouldn't always be. Every day was a gift.

The next day I drove Aunt Rose to Lambert International Airport to catch an afternoon flight. She needed to get back to San Diego to attend to personal matters that had piled up during her two-week absence. On my return from the airport, I visited Mom, knowing I could only stay an hour or two before heading off to work. After signing in at the lobby desk, I spotted Sylvia filling out charts at the nurses' station. I told her the story about the lucky nickel.

"I appreciate the excellent care Mom and all these people receive under your supervision," I said.

"It's all very well to thank us for caring for them," said Sylvia.

"Did I offend you?" I asked.

"No, we nurses do appreciate an occasional 'thank you' or other nice comments. But the real challenge is to get our residents to love us. It's a privilege to work with the elderly in the last stages of their lives."

"The elderly do teach us a lot about life and death," I said.

"To the deepest yearnings of the human heart," said Sylvia.

When I walked into Mom's apartment, Nurse Gigi was there, giving Mom her meds. As Mom was swallowing pills, I said, "Gigi, did you know my Mom made the second-highest marks of her entire high school class?"

"Wow. That is impressive," said Gigi.

Pride warmed Mom's face, but she made no attempt to invite more praise or brag about her accomplishments. She possessed so much internal strength that she required very few commendations from outside sources.

"My mother brought me up not to brag about myself," I said, "So I brag about my parents, my three sisters, and two daughters."

"It speaks well of a person when bragging about oneself does not come naturally," said Gigi.

"Maybe I will break my own rule just once. Does anyone care to hear about the day I received an award for perfect attendance all four years in high school?"

Gigi laughed. She seemed to appreciate my sense of humor. "Audrey, what is one thing I can get or do that will make today better for you?" she said, turning to Mom.

"Besides a miracle or hearing that one of my children hit the lottery, another blanket would be great," said Mom.

There is the phenomenon of miracles—remarkable events that apparently contradict known scientific laws. I believe in them. They are spoken of with reverence at hospitals and care facilities by nurses and doctors, who hold that often when things look the darkest, something unexplained happens and a very sick person is restored to health.

"That's an easy enough request to fulfill," said Sylvia. "The blanket part, I mean."

"You have a very nice way of treating the residents," said Mom.

"Well, it seems like everyone asks, 'How are you feeling?' when everyone knows the answer is 'bad.' I try not to do that. I just want people to know that I care, and that I'll do everything I can to make you happy and comfortable."

"I think I'm going to like you, Gigi," said Mom.

Gigi was the newest nurse in the unit. She had traveled to Bethesda from a small community in Michigan to visit her mother-in-law, a resident, but then decided to stay and help care for her by accepting an open nurse's position. She was the first nurse to help our family adjust to the new setting at Bethesda. She helped convince Mom to continue on with the rehab program after she moved to the assisted living side of the facility, in hopes of improving her balance, strength, and functionality. As she explained it, the more of these you have, the more independent you can be. Gigi's beautiful personality and calm demeanor always was appreciated by the residents. Along with Mom's other nurses Sylvia and Iesha, Gigi became a trusted advocate for our family in Mom's care. These three women cared, and their concern and understanding was evident in their voice and demeanor and in the kind things they did for the residents.

I liked the people who worked at Bethesda. They all knew how to live a life of no regret and never had to ask themselves questions about why they were wasting their lives. They were always on the lookout for the real needs of the residents and better ways in which they could help.

My visits to Bethesda were teaching me how to focus on my future. I was learning a lot about living healthier. I learned from the kitchen staff that I needed to take a vacation from processed foods and start to eat more naturally. One of the kitchen workers taught me that eating a banana will help you sleep and help lower your blood pressure, and the peel is good for shining your shoes. From Mable, the cleaning lady, I learned that a box of baking soda can freshen up the smell of your refrigerator, and a half teaspoon of it blended in a cup of water can help clear your sinuses if you drink the mixture. She taught me that you can clean almost anything with a mixture of lemon juice, water, and baking soda and that adding a tablespoon of vinegar to a load of wash will keep clothes and towels soft and fluffy without smelling like a salad. She showed me that vinegar is also a great product for banishing ants at an entryway and helping vegetables grow in a garden.

"Eat honey," Mable told me one day, "because it's good for you. If you eat honey and drink juice made from a blend of all the ripe vegetables in the garden, you'll combat the hardening and narrowing of your arteries. It's also good for sore throats, insomnia, and indigestion."

Mom chuckled, and I asked if I had missed something funny.

"No," said Mom, "but hearing you talk about honey reminds me of a funny conversation I had with Virginia the other morning. We were having breakfast, you see."

"Tell me. Were you talking about bees and honey?" I asked.

"I was just spreading honey on my toast, and Virginia was eating some cereal. She said she wanted to point out one small thing about her choice of Rice Krispies for breakfast. 'Do you hear the sounds coming from the inside of this bowl? Virginia asked as she poured the milk on her cereal. 'Do you mean the snap, crackle, and pop sounds?' I said. 'Exactly,' said Virginia. 'Would you like to know what they remind me of this morning?'

"Every person my age or older remembers those Rice Krispies commercials with the catchy 'snap, crackle, and pop' tune," I said.

"Well, Virginia compared the current White House administration to the sounds of Rice Krispies in a bowl of milk. She said Senate Majority Leader Harry Reid should have the nickname 'Snap' because he is fast to snap back at Republicans who voice opinions that denounce his way of thinking. She said the vice-president should have the nickname 'Crackle' because he likes to crack jokes about people who disagree with him. And finally, and I do mean finally, she said President Obama should have the nickname 'Pop' because he is like a father to 'Snap' and 'Crackle,' the two sons he never had in real life." Mom threw back her head and had a good laugh at Virginia's analogy, and Mabel and I laughed with her. It was great seeing Mom laughing again.

A day or two later, I again found myself walking down the hall to Mom's apartment. The door was unlocked, and I walked in. She was sitting in her comfy green chair.

"Good morning, Mom. How's everything?" I said.

"Okay," said Mom.

"I stopped at a truck farmer's stand on the way here. I brought you a cantaloupe, three ripe tomatoes, and a newspaper."

"Thank you," said Mom, as I set the goods on the coffee table.

"I tried calling earlier, but the nurse said you were down at rehab doing chair exercises."

"I was. I'm trying to trick my mind out of thinking about all these bruises I have on my arms. I thought exercise might do me some good."

"Are the bruises caused by the nurses checking your blood sugar or giving you shots?" I asked.

"Both. A few are probably from bumping into things, too. I know I bumped into the wall on the way to the bathroom last night," said Mom.

"Be careful," I said.

"Well, I know, but a woman's got to do, what a woman's got to do. Have you been busy at work?"

"You know how it is, Mom. The work never goes away. Customers always want something. I wish I was rich enough to retire today, so I could quit working, buy plane tickets, and take you to Ireland and trace your ancestors."

"You're funny. They're your ancestors too," said Mom. "You can't just claim the Scrubby Dutch ancestors from you father's side of the family. I'm just glad you visit me and bring me surprises," said Mom.

"Funny you mention that, because I do happen to have a surprise for you today."

"You do?" said Mom, her face lighting up.

"It's sort of refurbished surprise, because someone else already gave it to you once."

"I don't understand," said Mom. "You're being very mysterious."

"You'll understand when you see it."

"Well, Christmas is a long time coming. Give over. Is it that thing you're trying to hide behind your back?"

"I grinned and produced the package I was holding—a bag containing Dad's love letter to Mom, now nicely framed for her, with a photo of her and Dad when they were young also in the frame at the bottom of the letter.

She opened the bag, and tears came to her eyes. "I remember this," she said.

"I'm sure you do. Dad gave you this on your fiftieth wedding anniversary. He read it aloud to all of us, at the celebration."

"He was all choked up."

"He was indeed. As I am probably going to be if I read it to you now. May I at least give a try?"

Mom nodded solemnly.

I cleared my throat, held the letter up to the light, and began to read my father's words: "All I can say is that life with you has been a joy. It's hard to say what I love most about you—your patience, your laugh, your dimples, or your sense of humor. So many good things go into making you who you are that it's hard to pinpoint just one thing. Even during the tough times, life was easier because of you. Because you were a good listener, and because you have such a positive attitude, my life was better, and anything seemed possible with you near my side. Our love will last forever. George."

Now the tears were spilling down Mom's cheeks. I grabbed a couple of Kleenex and handed them to her.

"There was no one like your father," she said. "I was privileged to be his wife."

"Well, obviously he felt he was the one who was privileged. I'd say you both were."

"It was a good marriage," said Mom.

"You'll be together again," I said. "Love is one of the few things that lasts beyond the grave."

"Isn't that true," said Mom.

"Would you like me to set this over here where your guests can see it?"

"I'd like to just hold it for a while. We can put it over there later."

I handed her the frame, and she hugged it to her chest. I could tell she was still feeling emotional.

"I think I'll head down to the kitchen and see if they've got any snacks we might like," I said, wanting an excuse to leave the room and give Mom some private time.

"Cookies would be nice," said Mom, trying to sound conversational, but I could see there were still tears in her eyes.

Chapter 6

Our family paid six-thousand dollars a month for the services provided by the Bethesda team, for Mom to stay in her assisted living apartment, for whatever time she had left on this Earth. She was spared the noise and havoc of suburban life, the maze of dealing with traffic, the energy required to do housework, the responsibility of overseeing yard work, the hassle of paying the bills, the nuisance of shopping for groceries, the decisions of what to cook for meals, and some of the other basic chores and responsibilities of everyday living. The thing Mom loved most about assisted living was that she didn't have to worry about keeping track of all the medications she took everyday. She also loved the cleanliness and the décor of the entire complex.

Karen, with her special knack for design, had made it her goal to decorate Mom's apartment beautifully. Although Mom had already moved in and the major pieces of furniture were already in place, Karen couldn't stop adding little things to make Mom's quarters nicer still.

"Did you notice the bouquet of flowers I brought Mom?"

asked Karen one afternoon, appearing in the doorway of Mom's apartment.

"I did notice a nice scent in here," I said. "Now I see the vase, next to the lamp on the table. It adds a nice touch."

"You are such a guy," said Karen. "It's better if you notice things and offer compliments to a girl before you are asked about them."

"Sorry. Maybe if you had given me a little more time, I might have offered you a compliment," I said.

"Mom, I'm on my way to work, but I wanted to pick up your laundry," said Karen.

"Good. The basket's full and in the bathroom," said Mom. "Thank you, Karen."

"How soon do you want your clothes back?"

"Take your time. I have enough clean things for another week."

"I love you, Mom," said Karen, hugging and kissing her on the cheek. "I'd better leave, so I'm not late for work. Steve, let me know if you need help with anything."

"I will," I said.

"I love you, brother," said Karen.

"I love you, too," I said.

Kathy's sense of design and sense of color was amazing. The new patterned bedspread matched the beautiful brown tones in the new loveseat, and a crystal lamp that she picked out on the Internet showed the flair of a professional decorator. She had the three items shipped to the apartment from a furniture distribution center in St. Louis called "Weekends Only." The new purchases brought a balance and coordination to the carpeting and drapes. Everything went well together, and the rooms felt integrated, but Karen continued to alter and improve the appearance of the apartment. A pillow she had not been completely pleased with would disappear and be replaced with another of a different fabric and color, one that matched the shades of other accessories better. Glasses, cups, and plates would vanish, and the insides of the kitchen cabinets would blossom with sets of red-and-blue dinnerware. A flimsy picture frame, a cheap coaster, a worn old blanket would suddenly not be there, and something nicer would appear in its place. Karen had an eye for perfecting the look of a room, bringing together old heirlooms with practical modern conveniences, like when she decided to replace the vinyl coverings on a table and chest with eloquent lace draping. She made sure that the items most important to Mom were easily reachable in the top chest drawer, positioned across from her bed. A prayer book, several embroidered handkerchiefs, a hair brush, clean underwear, and an apron were the personal items that counted the most.

The apartment was orderly, empty of all the unnecessary accumulation from decades of everyday family living. Many items were recognizable, but Karen's new compositions made the space in the apartment look better than it did at the old house.

All this decorating and all these colors had me thinking about the furniture I had arranged in my own house in recent months. A fringe benefit of managing properties, as

I do, is getting to look over interesting things people place on the top of trash thrown into commercial dumpsters. Often chairs and other pieces of furniture are discarded because owners aren't interested in paying for repairs, don't have the knowledge or skills to do it themselves, or have decided to remodel their entire space. I liked wood furniture—the older the better. So I kept an eye open for wood furniture that was tossed away but only required minor fixes, such as a chair needing a few screws to repair an arm rest, a coffee table needing super glue to stabilize a wobbly leg, or an oak chest needing an inexpensive new back panel. It suddenly hit me that all the furniture I had repaired in the last year, I had spray-painted black. It's true that black paint is easy to use because it easily covers other colors in one coat, but maybe painting everything with the darkest hue on the color chart was a little morose. I made a mental note, promising myself that in the future I would follow the lead of my sisters, and try to add a little color to my surroundings.

So when I discovered a wooden coat rack placed next to a dumpster the next night while making my rounds, I decided to haul it home. The coat rack was broken. Its base was wobbly, the four large decorative hooks were loose, and the finish needed staining. Over the years every garment hung and removed had twisted and loosened the parts a little, until the last item to grace the coat rack made it unusable. The next morning, another glance at the pedestal showed me its secret; a tapered peg attached to a wedge needed some glue and an extra few turns to balance the base. I used a brownish-orange stain to cover the worn spots in the finish, first brushing the coat rack upright, then giving it another coat after placing it horizontally on old newspapers on my garage floor. Three coats later, all the blemishes were undetectable and the finish was smooth as glass. After new screws were re-fastened to the four hooks, the coat rack looked good as new.

One of Mom's favorite places to sit was in the library at Bethesda. It was always a pleasure for me to visit the library with her, to read a few chapters in a book, or just to stare at all the decorative things people had donated to the library. On a bookshelf over the fireplace was a piece of black-and-turquoise volcanic rock. Modern art, ceramic statues, small antiques, and even a totem were part of the arrangement. There were fresh-cut bouquets of flowers and, in a triangular glassed frame, a beautiful American flag, the stars perfectly aligned in the casing to accent its glory.

"Mom, I have something for you," I said, the day after the finish on the coat rack had dried. "I forgot to bring it in when I got here. Let me go get it out of my truck."

"I'm not going anywhere," said Mom, who was sorting through library books.

As I walked back in with the coat rack in hand, Mom clasped her hands together and said, "It's beautiful. Where did you get it?"

"I found it and refurbished it. Now when Helen and any of your other friends visit, they'll have a place to hang their jacket or coat."

"Thank you. I love it. When Karen was here last time, she polished all the wood in the apartment. Now with the coat rack, everything will shine."

"Have you picked out any good books to read?" I asked.

"When Helen was here, she rummaged around these shelves and suggested I read a novel called *Damage Control*. Ever heard of it?"

"It is written by New York Times bestselling author J. A. Jance," I said, picking up the book lying on the library table.

"Well, I haven't started reading it yet, but Helen told me it was about an Arizona sheriff in charge of investigating two complex cases," said Mom.

"Sounds suspenseful," I said.

"Helen ate breakfast with me that morning. Our server brought us each a plate of French toast and a box of honey-nut oats cereal. She asked, "Are you two ladies ready to start your morning bright and heart-healthy and full of energy?"

"How did you answer?" I asked.

"Helen didn't say anything, and I rolled my eyes," said Mom. "Then the server read from the back of the box, 'Eating grains, like oats, can boost your metabolism and keep you feeling full, longer. Keep grazing!' I said, 'We could have done without the "keep grazing" part at the end. Telling us to keep grazing makes it sound like you are talking to two fat cows."

"What did the server say to that?" I asked.

"She said, 'I'm sorry, ladies. I was just reading from

the box. I didn't mean to offend you.' That's when Helen spoke up. "Audrey didn't mean anything by her comment," she said. "She was teasing you. You can't offend two old gals like us that easily."

A good and genuine friend is a great comfort, and Helen was just such a friend to Mom. Her caring was a blessing to our entire family.

I carried Mom's book for her, and we meandered down the hallway to her apartment. No sooner had we got there than Helen popped into the room.

"Speaking of the devil," said Mom.

"What? Should my ears be ringing?" asked Helen.

"Mom was just telling a funny story about you and her," I said.

"Funny story? I can tell you a funny story," said Helen. "One day a couple of months ago your mother called and said there was another casino trip brewing and we should go, so she signed us up," said Helen, beginning her story. Ever since their husbands had died, Mom or Helen had been in the habit of taking a chartered bus with a group of other seniors to a casino in the small town of Pana, Iowa. They liked playing the nickel-poker machines, especially when they came home with more money than they left with.

"We had an interesting time," said Helen. "On the way there, the bus driver drove three-and-a-half hours without stopping."

"A woman bus driver would have scheduled one or two stops along the way," said Mom.

"All that driver talked about was the swollen rivers. A female driver would have known not to point out the bladder conditions of a river to old ladies who need to use the bathroom," said Helen.

"It started to rain and then we *really* had to use the bathroom," said Mom. "When the bus driver finally did stop, we both had already peed in our pants."

"That's not very funny," I said.

"Oh pshaw, that's not the funny part," said Helen. "The funny part came after we checked into the hotel when I had to call the front desk and tell them to send paramedics to our room."

"What?" I said. "Mom, you never told me about this."

Mom was blushing.

"I told the clerk, my friend here is naked," said Helen, ignoring my interruption. "She fell down in the shower, and can't get up."

Now Mom was chuckling. "Helen took a picture of the two young paramedics helping me stand up in the shower. Thank God she waited until they gave me a towel to wrap around myself before she took the picture," said Mom.

"I guess your mother was trying to show her vulnerable side," said Helen. "Those paramedics were pretty cute."

"Maybe Mom was practicing to audition for a job as an underwear model," I said.

"At my age," Mom said, "the only underwear anyone would let me model is Depends."

"We did manage to have a good time on that casino trip," said Helen.

Their mishaps manifested as funny instead of distressing whenever Mom or Helen regaled me with stories at their own expense. They both had a wonderful attitude and were determined to find the fun and the humor in life, refusing to play the role of victim, despite their declining health and growing challenges. It was that kind of attitude that kept them fun to be around and young at heart. "This is the way I want to grow old," I thought to myself. My Mom, Helen, and Aunt Rose were modeling the way for me and my sisters.

Chapter 7

Five years before Mom moved to Bethesda, while recovering from major heart surgery, she received a letter in the mail from her insurance company. I never told her about it because she had enough to worry about getting treatments for complications of a bacterial infection from a quadruple by-pass and heart-valve replacement. The letter read:

Dear Ms. Audrey M. Hubele:

Please note that a Summons and Complaint concerning an important matter may be filed and served upon you in the near future. In the event you do receive a lawsuit by mail or in person, be certain to note who was served and the date, time, and method of service on a separate piece of paper. Please attach this information to the lawsuit and forward it immediately to me in the enclosed envelope.

It is important that you forward to us the lawsuit as soon as possible as the law requires that a response be filed within twenty-one days of receipt of the Summons and Complaint. Because of the time limits imposed, we request that you forward any lawsuits within two days of receipt. Your failure to do so may jeopardize our ability to provide you with a defense.

Keep this letter so you will have my name and phone number for future reference. Please call should you have any questions. Thank you in advance for your cooperation.

The letter puzzled me. Mom had never been involved in a legal dispute. The closest thing she'd ever had to "trouble with the law" was a speeding ticket she got at age twenty-four, for going two miles over in a thirty-mile speed zone. Twenty-six days after the mysterious letter appeared, another one arrived:

Dear Audrey M. Hubele:
We received the Summons and Complaint Joseph XXXXX vs. Audrey M. Hubele. Your insurance policy with Safeco Insurance Company provides a defense, and the case has been referred to our lawyers. The lead attorney assigned to your case will be contacting you soon. If you need to reach your defense attorney before that time, you may do so by calling and speaking with the managing attorney of the case, Maryann XXXXX.

Your representation by our lawyers is limited to defending the claims that are raised in the complaint. We will pay for the reasonable costs of defense, including the fees and costs of our lawyers. Our lawyers will not be advising Safeco Insurance Company about whether they provide coverage for your case.

The plaintiff asks for unspecified damages against you. The Coverage under your policy with us is limited to $50,000.00 for damages to any one person and/or $100,000.00 for all damages arising from one occurrence. Any damages awarded against you in excess of these limits will be your responsibility. If you have any concerns, you may want to consult a personal attorney.

You may be eligible for reimbursement of expenses you incur at our request. Please review your policy for specific details of these supplementary payments.

If you wish, you have the right to retain a personal attorney, at you own expense, to join in representing you. If so, we would be glad to have your attorney work with us in preparing for and defending the lawsuit. If you or your personal attorney, should you retain one, have any questions, concerns or disagreements with the direction your defense is taking, you should convey those concerns to me immediately. The lawyers will require your assistance in preparing your defense. They will ask you for any documents related to the claim. In addition, your defense attorney will prepare you if you are deposed and will defend your deposition. If this case goes to trial, the lawyers will meet with you in advance for a detailed discussion. In the interim, you should not discuss this matter with anyone other than the attorney preparing your defense or representatives of Safeco Insurance Company.

If you become aware of new information concerning

*this case, if you leave the area for more than a few days,
or if you change your address or telephone number,
please advise us immediately. If you have any additional
questions or concerns, please feel free to contact me.*

With this letter, it all came back to me, and I knew who
it was suing Mom. The incident in question happened on
the evening of April 1, 2006. The date was easy to recall,
because it seemed like a cruel April fool's joke. Apparently
Mom had visited Dad's grave at Jefferson Barracks Cemetery that morning. Upon driving home, she stopped her
car on an incline a few feet behind another vehicle at an
intersection, waiting for the light to change. Suddenly, the
rearview mirror glued to her front windshield lost its grip
and fell into Mom's lap. This startled her, causing her foot
to slip off the pedal and the car to slightly roll forward,
bumping the car in front of her at a speed of less than one
mile per hour. Mom and the driver of the other vehicle
pulled into an adjacent parking lot. Inspecting both vehicles, Mom could see there was no damage to either car,
but the other driver, Joseph XXXXX, insisted on calling
the police. Mom waited, and when the police arrived, they
put in their report that neither vehicle had been damaged.
Mom had an uneasy feeling about the incident, as the
unreasonable behavior of the other driver made her suspect he was up to something. She insisted I take a picture
of the front of her car, just in case. She said the other driver
was "a weasel" who seemed like the type of guy who
would sue any person for any trivial reason.

Mom's intuition was right, because the weasel was suing Mom. He was trying to make a fast buck by taking advantage of an elderly woman and our court system.

A few days after I opened the second letter, the lawyers representing the case sent interrogatories and request forms for production of documents. Acting as power of attorney for my mother, I had to respond to the matter. At first I didn't know where to start. I was worried that if I didn't make sense of the documents soon and respond quickly, I might miss some deadline and make matters worse for Mom. It took me hours to complete, but I immediately got to work filling out the paperwork and getting everything notarized. I couldn't believe the weasel had the nerve to lie at the expense of an elderly woman.

One month after sending everything in, I received a phone call from the lawyer for Mom's insurance company. He recommended that we offer the plaintiff $1,400 to settle the case. He explained that if we did not settle, we could easily incur $1,400 just in expenses. I wanted to scream. All this fuss about a fraudulent lawsuit, while my Mom was fighting for her life. Mom had actually fallen into a coma, which she stayed in for five days. The last thing in the world I needed to be thinking about just then was this silly lawsuit.

"Is this letter for real?" I thought. "Are these people for real? Why do some people bear the entire burden, while others only want to take advantage?" Worse than an athlete scoring points and then taunting a player on the opposing team, worse than an adult screaming at a young girl working retail because her service is too slow, worse than a teenage boy stealing a set of hubcaps from a car, is a con man taking advantage of an elderly woman. This case was at the top of my detestable list.

On August 8, 2008, another letter arrived in my mailbox:

Dear Mr. Steve Hubele:
I am pleased to report that your mother's case has settled for $1,500. This is a favorable result, one that could not have been obtained without your help. The assistance you provided was greatly appreciated. You will not need to do anything further. I will advise you when the case is closed with the Court. The wrapping-up process takes approximately one month. Until then, if you have any questions, please contact me.

I filed away that last letter along with the other letters. "I hope some day Joseph XXXXX becomes a man," I thought. For several days I secretly hated the weasel who had sued my mother, whoever he was and wherever he lived. For the next six weeks, Mom received treatments every day to fight the complications of the bacteria infection. I never told her about the court case.

One day after Mom had been living at Bethesda for several weeks, she said, "Steve, we need to make a present for the staff. They have been so good to me." This seemed like an excellent idea, and I was surprised I hadn't thought of it myself.

"You're right," I said. "We should. What do you think you'd like to give them?"

"How about one of those nice gift baskets, like people give you at Christmas?"

"Wonderful idea!"

I visited a nearby gift shop that made up baskets of this sort, but the price tags were outrageous. I figured I could put a similar basket together, but with a larger variety of items, for about one-third the price. I drove to Michael's, a craft store in the neighborhood, and bought a nice woven cane basket with a sturdy handle for twelve dollars. I drove to the grocery store and painstakingly selected four of the best-looking pieces of fruit from each pyramid pile on display—oranges that shone their full color; bananas that had survived transport without any bruising; peaches at their peak ripeness; and crisp, colorful pears. I figured the basket I bought had more than enough room for all the hand-selected pieces of fruit. After leaving the grocer's, I drove across the road to the Panera Bread shop and purchased four sourdough bagels and four packets of garlic-herb cheese spread. Once I finished shopping for all the items I needed, I drove back to Bethesda and solicited Mom's approval in carefully arranging the basket.

"That is some great-looking fruit," said Mom. "The nurses and other employees at the hospital will devour everything in that basket before the end of their next coffee break."

The only thing still left in the process was to shrink-wrap some cellophane around the outside of the basket to secure the items inside. Using plastic wrap and Mom's portable hair dryer, I manufactured a tight seal. The end product looked delicious and inviting.

I walked to the front desk and dropped off the basket at the nurses' station. This was just one of many lessons I learned from my mother, to thank people who help you. Simple gestures along the way mean a great deal to people who genuinely put their heart into their work, like the staff at Bethesda. They deserve to be acknowledged for their contribution, and despite all the issues in her own life Mom had to worry about, she managed to think of those who cared for her and found a way to express gratitude. Needless to say, the staff did appreciate the gesture. And I'm pretty sure the goodies did disappear by the end of the next coffee break, as Mom had predicted.

I had noticed that Mom now preferred to wear only a few outfits from her wardrobe. She wanted to wear things that were comfortable and had extra pockets. She often wore a dark blue blazer because it had pockets on the outside and the inside, and nothing else in her closet gave her the utilitarian convenience of this piece of clothing. Wearing this jacket freed her hands to walk with her cane and to hold a glass of orange juice with the other hand.

"I think you like your dark blue blazer," I said one day. "You wear it a lot."

"I don't have to carry a heavy purse when I wear it," said Mom. "Women are always taught to accept a little pain in the pursuit of beauty. I say the heck with that. At my age, I'm only interested in ergonomics. I can keep my wallet, cell phone, credit card, lip gloss, reading glasses, and keys in all the extra pockets of my blazer without any extra weight to bear on one shoulder or the other."

"I take it you're not interested in trying to find a part-time job as a fashion consultant?" I asked. "I think sleeveless floral prints are coming back."

"No, I don't think so. No to answer your question, and no to your statement," said Mom. "A person can still be totally trendy and fashion-forward without exposing every part of their body."

"If you feel like you have nailed your look, and you're comfortable, that's all that matters," I said.

Every time a caretaker thinks they have a little free time, and how wonderful it is to enjoy free time, something happens to sadden you, push you harder, worry you, or force you to think and find a way to fix a problem. But occasionally you are encouraged or entertained. Mom's famous sense of humor buoyed me up, and her strongly felt opinions on almost every subject also made me chuckle from time to time. "Ambition dwindles with age, and so does energy and enterprise," she told me one day. "There are far too many young people in America who think working a ten-hour day with no social life on weekdays is some kind of evil punishment. They look at work as an ailment that will send them to the infirmary."

"I'm afraid to admit it," I said, "but I'm not twenty-years-old anymore either. The physical labor entailed in doing my job is getting harder as I get older."

"Wait until you get to be my age," said Mom.

Long conversations were often enough to tire Mom. Sometimes, after a short morning visit and still in her nightgown and robe, she would shuffle into her bedroom, climb into bed, and go back to sleep. She claimed that most of her dreams were about my dad. She could feel him lying beside her, close enough that she could feel his presence. Sometime she'd dream of the way they used to dance together, him pulling her down to dip, her heart beating a little faster when he put his hands on her waist and lifted her up.

Mom once told me, "I learned to praise my husband about all the good things I loved about him instead of always pouncing on him about little things that really didn't matter. After coming to that realization, it was liberating not to always be worrying about dirty dishes, soiled laundry, and unwanted clutter. Eventually we learned to read the newspaper together in the morning and work together to complete the chores later in the day."

When my father died, my mother and I stood to the side of his coffin to greet the people who came and waited in a long line to say their farewells. By staying strong for my mother, I believed my resolve served to keep her and my three sisters from crying all day. I was going to cry for my father, but later and alone, and behind locked doors. Of all the relatives Dad had, most of the uncles, aunts, cousins, and nephews who had shared the good times of his youth at picnics and family gatherings seemed to have forgotten him over the years, yet here so many of them were at his funeral. To me, the voices of such relatives and old friends sounded false, like voices out of the shadows. But maybe the problem was with my point of view. I'm older now and realize how fast the months and years actually pass. In the bustle of living, it's easy to lose contact with people you actually care about, always meaning to touch base sometime but never getting around to it. The fact that so many people came to Dad's funeral was a testimony to the fact that he was respected and loved—even by people he had not heard from in years.

Soon after my father died, I realized Mom was having a hard time adjusting. I knew she found the greatest amounts of grief flooding over her at night, when she turned her face into the pillow and cried herself to sleep.

For most people going through the mourning process, the grieving is all-encompassing at first. Then, slowly, they adjust and move on. But sometimes, for reasons that doctors and scientists still don't know, mourning lingers and intensifies for some people. Grief was complicated for Mom. She couldn't see any way of going on happily without her husband. Every day of that first year of bereavement was a chore trying to keep her interested in something, in anything. Mired in sadness, she stared out windows for long periods of time, quit reading, stop watching TV, ignored phone calls, slept too much, and lived a self-imposed life of isolation. She turned down invitations, and most of her friends—confused and frustrated that she seemed to be refusing to move on—stopped calling her. But not Aunt Rose and not Mom's friend Helen. Both women kept calling once a week to check on her and pound heavy blows of support her way, partly because they themselves had experienced the pain of losing husbands and understood the emotions Mom was grappling with.

Helen told Mom she found it helpful to take up a meditative hobby after her husband died. She had learned to knit. First blankets, then scarves, then hats and socks, from patterns she found in books at the library. Helen wasn't alone in finding a hobby she loved. Almost all of the residents at Bethesda regularly take part in at least one crafting activity, whether it's knitting or felting items from yarn, fashioning coffee mugs from clay, glazing complicated puzzle layouts, or piecing together floral arrangements.

Our elderly generation has always appreciated the satisfaction of making things and the security of being able to use self-taught skills to provide for their families. When men went overseas to fight the war, almost every woman at home had a hand in supporting the cause of freedom, whether it was helping treat injured soldiers brought back from the battlefield, supporting the USO, helping sell War Bonds, or working in factory making parts for tanks and airplanes. The manufacturing boom following World War II caused crafting to become a pastime instead of a necessity because people no longer needed to make everything they used in their daily lives. But the habit of making things by hand stuck with my parents' generation, as did their respect for anything crafted with skill and care.

At first Mom and I talked openly about our memories of Dad. But because Mom had temporarily checked out from the world, I started being more careful about mentioning his name. If it slipped out inadvertently, her sensitivities would erupt through the expressions on her face. One day I said to her:

"I'm tired of only talking about Dad, Mom. We need to move on. We are in no worse shape than any other family who loses a husband or father through death."

"Your father was no ordinary husband or father," Mom answered. "You may be ready to let him go, but I'm not." Her voice trembled a little, and her pain stayed there. But I was determined to convincing my mother to let go of the past and to find a way to make the most of the rest of her life.

I needed to allow Mom to talk about Dad. Explanations from me like, "He's in a better place" or "God has a grand plan for you," were unnecessary. Mom needed a listening ear. By me listening more, she eventually grew tired of grieving her past, present, and future with my dead father. I learned to play a supporting role, instead of a central role, because grief belongs to the griever. I realized that trying to fix the unfixable is a mistake. And Mom realized some relief from having a son who refused to take her pain away by forcing her to grieve in a certain way. I had to stay willing to witness her searing, unbearable pain.

A care partner bears witness and is present alongside a loved one to tackle projects even when it feels like you are sinking into a deep hole.

It was a long journey, but in time, Mom did recover and begin to involve herself in life again. Patience, determination, and expressions of love from Aunt Rose during many long talks on the phone are what finally brought Mom out of the doldrums of her grief.

Chapter 8

For several months, I visited Mom every Wednesday and on weekends, and a home nurse checked on her on Tuesdays and Thursdays, sometimes phoning me to give suggestions about medical equipment or supplies, and when to make a run to the pharmacy for medications or personal hygiene products. Most aspects of my visits were becoming routine, until on a grey afternoon in June, I walked in and found Mom sitting in her favorite recliner and wearing what looked a lot like a Santa hat. It was some kind of white and red knitted thing that she had it pulled low around her ears. She was sipping eggnog and still in her pink satin pajamas.

I warmed some coffee, poured it into a cup, and added a little eggnog as a topper. I sat on the couch in the living room across from Mom and drank my special mixture, as Mom's gaze travelled around the room.

"Gone to nothing," Mom said, "like a scarecrow that stays in one spot all day, watching all the birds fly free and the rabbits run free."

"Gone to nothing . . . are you losing weight, Mom?"

"Yeah, and none of my clothes fit anymore. That's one of the reasons I'm still in my pajamas."

"Watching your recovery has been a beautiful thing to witness, like watching an overweight child ride a bicycle for the first time," I said. "Then he starts training because he likes it so much."

"That is a bad example. You make me sound like a clumsy clog, and you forget I have lost weight," she said. "All my life I was somewhat athletic, at least with bowling and playing golf."

"I'm sorry. I guess a man should know better than to mention weight to a woman," I said. "I should have used a golf analogy."

The holiday was a long ways off, but Mom's hat and the eggnog made me think of Christmas. Holidays can be hard for the elderly. They bring up memories of happier times. Mom looked happier than when I had first walked into the apartment, and I told her that seeing her there made me remember Christmases at her house and how she always wrote a script for the grandkids to perform. There were no tears and no tissues when Mom went all-in working on one of her skits. Every year, when her writing was finished and all the props were ready, she would pronounce, "Now it's Christmas." Because of her little productions, it was impossible not to remember the spirit and true meaning of the holiday. Her plays always put family members in a good mood. The chocolate chip cookies, the eggnog, the presents, and the decorated tree that accumulated ornaments each year only accented that meaning for our family. Every play was performed within the cozy confines of the living room at the old House, and every family member was expected to participate.

Mom wrote and directed her version of a popular Christmas play every holiday season for nearly a decade. *A Christmas Carol, Twelve Days of Christmas, The Nutcracker, The Little Match Girl, The Elves and the Shoemaker,* and *A Snowy Day* are scripts she worked especially hard on to spread family cheer and goodwill during six separate Christmas Day celebrations. Her plays always told a story about the proper way a person is supposed to behave during special or trying moments.

In the last years when Mom prepared her house for Christmas, her spirit sparkled. Her blood pressure had stabilized enough that her doctors had cleared her to perform light chores around the house up to ten minutes at a time, before needing to sit down to take a break. She was even back to reading books and reading the newspaper for a while, though the news often upset her. Mom was a staunch conservative with no use for the liberal agenda that she felt the local newspaper promoted.

Each year before the Christmas skit, Mom would regale the family with stories of Christmases from her childhood. "When I was six, my sister Joan was four, and my sister Rose was two," Mom would tell us. In 1936, we woke up Christmas morning, and under the tree were three doll-baby beds that my father had made. They were stained and varnished, and very shiny. My mother had sewn a mattress, sheets, a pillow, and a coverlet trimmed in red and green for each bed. In each bed was a brand-new doll. I wish I still had mine. Our house on Christmas Eve was always crowded. In the beginning, there were relatives from five generations.

"One Christmas Eve, I was waiting for my boyfriend George to arrive. A beautiful Christmas tree, the prettiest we ever had, stood in the corner of our living room. Hot chocolate was on the stove, and cookies were baking in the oven. A big snow storm the week before made it difficult for people traveling around. Neighbors shoveled snow for days. When George finally arrived, two hours late, he wanted to talk to me privately, but the only empty room was the bathroom. So he grabbed my hand and took me there. Then he knelt down on one knee, took hold of both of my hands, and asked me to marry him. I didn't speak right away, as tears started to run down both sides of my face. When I said 'yes,' he slipped a diamond ring on my finger. He stood up, threw his arms around me, and kissed me right there in the bathroom. That moment is my best Christmas memory."

Two years after my parents married, they bought their house. Family celebrated Christmas every year at that house. Memories of Christmas that were especially dear were the ones celebrated with grandchildren. Amanda, the first grandchild, would entertain the family singing into her microphone for hours at a time, and no one seemed to mind. Lindsay, the next grandchild, performed song-and-dance routines with Amanda. Allison, the third grandchild, not wanting to be outdone by her older sister and cousin, would often be assigned the lead role in Mom's play. When the first boy grandbaby, Bradley, came along, he played Baby Jesus in that year's play. Only a few weeks old at the time, he slept through the entire performance in his makeshift cradle. While Baby Jesus slept, Grandpa mouthed sound effects of animals in the manger, sometimes at the appropriate moment and sometimes not, and we laughed at all the silly outfits sewn together from rags and old towels. The best skit written and produced at the old house was the last one, "Christmas Blessings," with all six of Mom's grandchildren participating.

"Welcome to my endeavor," Mom began. "My angelic grandchildren will play their roles in proclaiming peace and good will. Hopefully they will bring good tidings and great joy to the rest of us, without complaining too much."

"'Angelic' is a bit of a stretch," I thought. "Truer to say 'generally pleasant.'"

"Sydney and Connor will play songs on the piano. My play is titled, 'Christmas Blessings,' and I hope you like it," said Mom.

It was nice to see Mom back and engaged with her grandchildren after suffering through a litany of health woes that would have depressed almost anyone else. She gave herself insulin shots every morning to control her diabetes and she swallowed eight pills every day to control heart-related issues. For years she had been giving up pieces of her life, but because she was still able to bathe, dress herself, and use the toilet without assistance, Mom wasn't ready for help from another person. She refused to be a burden to her children or grandchildren.

Growing up, I didn't always listen to Mom's Christmas plays with complete attention. That evening, I not only wanted to listen; I wanted to videotape the play so her grandchildren could watch it years later.

All the grandchildren had butterflies in their stomachs, but they all had fun participating. Amanda started the action by walking out from the kitchen holding a tray of food.

"Do you want turkey or ham, which would you like? If you behave, you can have both. Maybe I will bring you some nuts, cookies, cake, and candy later on. We can all diet tomorrow," said Amanda.

"Look at the Christmas tree standing tall. It sure does sparkle and shine. We bought the ornaments at the mall. Real Christmas trees are the best because of the pine smell. The tree this year is better than all those scraggly trees we had in other years," said Lindsay, reciting her lines.

"Oh, the joy of the Christmas decorations. Did everyone notice the one on the ceiling? I think Grandma exceeded our expectations this year," said Amanda. "The star on the ceiling sparkles and glistens and gets me reeling."

"All the elves are so elated, even knowing they can't yet sit down, more toys must be built and inflated, then delivered to every town," said Lindsay.

"Santa's sleigh slides swiftly through the night, over the mountains and down in the valleys. All the presents are wrapped tight. It's up to me and my fellow reindeers to get all the presents delivered in a timely fashion," said

Bradley, with a big red plastic ball fastened to his nose by an elastic string around his head.

"Notice all the burning candles around you; they sure do make things glow. Be sure not to sit on one; or you will surely say, HO, HO, HO!" said Sydney.

"I'm Rudolph the red-nosed reindeer, and this big red nose is quite a pain. Some people think my nose is red from drinking too much beer, but I beg to differ. I do abstain," said Bradley.

"Our Christmas presents are all in a line; and under the tree they lie, so hey! I hope that big one's mine; I certainly love this holiday," recited Connor.

"The snowman in the front yard has a hat, scarf, and some other thing, and he looks good enough to cuddle. Maybe some love and cheer he'll bring, 'cause we know he'll soon be just a big puddle," said Sydney.

"Maybe more snowflakes will fall on Christmas Day. Snow makes the world look brighter. On the ground, like diamonds if I may, they make Grandma's hair look whiter," said Connor.

"Santa Claus is a really nice old guy, and from his tasks he never ever tarries. He looks like he eats lots of pie, and he must finish his work, pooped from all the gifts he carries," said Bradley.

"Down the chimney on every street, and every Christmas, he goes. Just my luck,

Santa I will never meet, because I'll be sleeping, and afraid he'll get stuck," said Sydney, wearing a paper grocery bag colored to look like a chimney with red bricks.

"The best Christmas flower when all is said and done, in truth it's the poinsettia.

But be careful not to eat one, because it will upset ya," said Bradley.

"We all have memories of Grandpa, the man we were privileged to know. So, on behalf of Grandma, this play is dedicated to him," said Allison.

Noticing tears running down both sides of her grandmother's face, Amanda quickly spoke the last lines to end the play.

"Wait. Hold on, lest we forget the one whose birth we celebrate. We owe Him quite a debt. Let us all commemorate. Happy Birthday, Jesus, and Merry Christmas, everyone," said Amanda. "We celebrate the Virgin Mary bringing forth her first-born son, wrapping Him in swaddling clothes, and comforting Him in a manger, because others denied the holy family a room at the inn. And there were shepherds abiding in the field, keeping watch over their flock by night. And the angel said unto them, 'I bring you good tidings of great joy, which shall go to all people. Let's give glory to God in the highest, and on Earth peace, and good will toward men.'"

"We will end with Sydney and Connor playing the piano," said Bradley.

As the brother-and-sister duo played "Silent Night," the rest of the family sang along. When they played "Angels We Have Heard on High," everyone just listened.

After everyone had gone home that night except for me, I glanced at Mom. She was trying to maintain a calm expression, but I knew she was upset about something.

"What is it, Mom?" I asked her.

"I forgot to send out my charitable donations this year," said Mom. I wanted to keep sitting on the couch, but I knew what I had to do before I went home. I got up from the couch to look for a pen. Writing checks to charities at Christmas time gave Mom a feeling that she was helping the world.

"I can help you, Mom," I said. "Let's take care of it right now."

A few moments later, I was sitting at the kitchen table with Mom, as she went over her list.

"Send twenty-five dollars to the American Heart Association, twenty-five dollars to the Diabetes Foundation, and twenty-five dollars to the American Cancer Research Fund," said Mom.

"No one can accuse those three charitable organizations of disloyalty to worthy causes," I said.

"Send fifty dollars to the United Way and fifty dollars to the American Red Cross. I give more to those two because they oversee more causes, and both are known for conducting their businesses with honesty and integrity," said Mom. "And send twenty-five dollars to Heifer International."

Heifer International, headquartered in Little Rock, Arkansas, professes to work in the areas of livestock and agriculture to help develop programs that alleviate hunger and poverty. When Mom's mother died, Mom decided to honor her by making a donation to the organization, because Grandma had always loved animals. Heifer International works by sending two cows, two sheep, two oxen, or two beehives to families in poorer parts of the globe. If the animals have offspring, the families are supposed to pass on one or more of the newborns to another family in need. The idea is that every gift will multiply.

Because women in the poorest parts of the world are responsible for doing much of the food preparation for their families with limited resources, animals bring new energy, new ideas, and increased self-esteem to mothers and their children. Women who are facing gender discrimination are trained to transform themselves into powerful small-scale ranchers and businesswomen. That's the idea anyway.

I was suspicious of some of the claims made by the Heifer International organization. "Mom, have you ever looked at a copy of an annual report filed by these people?" I asked.

"No, but they admit in their brochures that they never use any money to track individual animals. They say doing that would waste precious dollars. They claim the money is always used to support the bigger mission, where it can do the most good to transform families and communities," said Mom.

Who was I to tell my mother how to spend her charitable giving dollars, if it made her happy to do so? If her donation had even a tiny chance of helping one little child in a faraway land, then that little child was worth saving. So I signed another check for twenty-five dollars made out to Heifer International in Mom's name.

That night on the way home, I dropped Mom's dona-tions into a mailbox. I had the feeling that our Christmas Eve that night was ending a tradition. Indeed it did, for that was Mom's last Christmas with us. I wondered whether all traditions eventually end. It was a very cold night. As I drove home, I remembered something Karen had told me on another Christmas Eve. "Jesus was born on this night," she said. "This is the only day in the calendar when everybody has hope. All men, women, and children are at peace. Jesus offers us hope." She was right, and I wished we could stay this way forever, but the day after Christmas would be different. Then we would hear about something bad that happened. Every Christmas Jesus was born, and it wasn't two-thousand years ago to Karen. She did her best to plant something of that peace in me.

Our family was lucky to have all the memories sparked by Mom's Christmas plays. At any time of the year, some-thing small—like a candle, a decoration, or a silly red-and-white hat—could trigger a memory about Christmas plays at the house Mom lived in for sixty years. The flashbacks are wonderful.

Chapter 9

One late afternoon, after spending a couple of hours paying bills, I called my mother to invite her out for dinner, and drove the eight miles to Bethesda to pick her up.

Then something unexpected happened. As I brought my truck around to the back entrance parking lot, there stood Mom standing on the sidewalk. She was holding a sweater in one hand and leaning on her cane with the other, ready and waiting to go somewhere, anywhere.

After I parked my truck and walked over to greet her, Mom practically fell into my arms and ordered me to help her walk and get into the truck's front seat. I knew she was eager to get out and have an experience that wasn't "hospital" but "normal." The constant flow of physicians subjecting her to batteries of tests for reflexes, eyesight, hearing, heart rate, and stability, and nurses hooking her up to machines and giving her shots were nuisances she wanted to get away from for a while.

"Sometimes the nurses want to have full conversations with me really early in the morning before I'm awake, but I know it is wrong to want to kill them," said Mom, as

I drove the truck up to the entrance of her wing of the building.

"I know you don't really mean that," I said. "Wait here for a minute while I go inside and tell Sylvia that we're going out for an hour or two."

"Okay," said Mom. "Remind her we'll be back before seven, for night medications. Don't forget to sign me out at the front desk."

I walked through the back door, took the elevator to the second floor, walked to the nurses' station, and told Sylvia what we were doing.

"Steve, I have something to tell you, too," said Sylvia. "Your mother is having some difficulty regarding her sense of time. She fell asleep within moments after getting her insulin shot after dinner last night. An hour after sunset, we found her walking down the hall."

"Where was she going?" I asked.

"She told me she was headed to the dining hall for breakfast. I tried to ease her embarrassment and walked with her back to her room. I told her she probably made the mistake because of the glare on the tree branches outside her window from the street lights. I told her the glare might have been mistaken for the brightness of the sun in early morning."

"Thank you for that, Sylvia," I said

"Have a good time with your Mom."

When I got back to the truck, Mom was waiting quietly with her hands clutching the top of her black shoulder purse.

"You gave me a turn, standing there on the sidewalk, Mom," I said. "You looked like you were getting ready to run away."

"Oh, go on with your driving," said Mom. "You know I wouldn't do that. I had already told both nurses that we were going out for dinner. I even told the new lady at the front desk I was waiting for my ride. She kept me in her sight the whole time I was waiting on the sidewalk."

"So where do you want to go for dinner?" I asked.

"I'm in the mood for seafood," said Mom.

"That's fine with me," I said. "Red Lobster it is, right?"

Mom was in a good mood. I had learned to gauge her mood, not from what she said or the expressions on her face, but from the way she moved. When she was happy, she walked better, with little hesitation in her stride. When things were not going well, she walked more slowly and did everything with less ease. Sometimes she just stopped, sat in her chair, and stared out the window of her apartment.

"You know me pretty good," she said. "I have a craving for a fish platter, maybe a salmon platter. Maybe we should order salads first," said Mom.

"Talking about food is making me hungry," I said.

"Most anything will make you hungry," said Mom.

"It's been a long time since we ate at Red Lobster, probably eight or nine months. There may be a wait this time of day, but the lobby has plenty of seating for customers."

One certain thing in an uncertain world is that people need to eat. One desire may come to fruition; another may fade into the sunset. The game of life throws you plenty of curve balls in unpredictable situations, but mealtimes come around in regular fashion. I was going to enjoy this dinner with Mom.

Surveying the traffic, I spotted a newly constructed office building to my left that had gone unnoticed to my eyes until now, and a bulldozer clearing a plot of land to my right. A beverage truck hauling Michelob and Budweiser beer in bottles rumbled past at probably fifty-five miles an hour, rattling the windows of my truck and the raw nerves of Mom and myself.

After stopping at the nearest gas station to fill the tank, we joined the traffic on the interstate for three miles. The breeze was light and the air was warm. It took us longer to get from the parking lot to our table than it did fighting the traffic from Bethesda to Red Lobster, but neither Mom nor I cared about the prologue. A change of scenery and fresh seafood occupied both of our minds.

The happy din of families and couples filled the restaurant. In the background, ice cubes clattered in glasses and silverware clanged against dishes. Waiters scurried back and forth in the aisles. The smells of the South overtook our other senses—fried breaded seafood, shrimp cocktail sauce, broccoli soup, fresh-baked bread, and the sweet-potato pie Red Lobster franchises in other parts of the country apparently don't offer the Southern options that our St. Louis Red Lobster offers, and we appreciated the added touch of the local cuisine being made available. This was definitely one of our favorite restaurants.

"Here comes our waitress." said Mom. "She looks serious, but awfully nice."

"How did you derive that information already?" I asked. "We haven't even talked to her yet."

"Hi, my name is Molly," said the young girl, approaching our table. "What can I get for you guys to drink?"

"Nice to meet you, Molly," said Mom. "My name is Audrey, and this is my son, Steve."

"Nice to meet you both," said Molly.

"I'll have an unsweetened iced tea with lemon, please," said Mom.

"Please make that two unsweetened iced teas with lemon," I said.

"Sure, I'll be right back."

"The wild rice pilaf with beans is so good here," said Mom. "Once you start, it's hard to stop eating that medley. But the beans make my digestive system act bad, if you know what I mean."

"Yes, I do know, and thank you for waiting until Molly left the table before making that remark," I said.

Watching Molly work other tables, we found out quickly that she was a born waitress. She identified the music playing in the background, updated patrons on the weather forecast, explained the history of the lithographs on the wall, and explained the specials for the night. She had a perfect radio voice, warm and clear. When two young men at another table asked her moronic questions, she answered politely, careful not to make fun of either man. She had a sense of humor, too.

"Are you going to throw our rolls to us?" asked one young man, probably in his early twenties.

"The heat or the humidity must have gotten to you," Molly answered. "The restaurant known as 'home of the thrown rolls' is in Sikeston. You guys are about three hours north of that establishment. That restaurant only knows three spices: salt, pepper, and ketchup. In that town, a traffic jam is ten cars on a two-lane road waiting to pass a tractor."

Actually, the section of Missouri that encompasses the towns of Sikeston and New Madrid is known by motorists as Little Dixie, because the inhabitants there talk a little funny. It's where you first notice the curious Southern dialect, because words are spoken as if they have extra vowels and consonants. In 1811, that part of the state unleashed an earthquake so powerful, the Mississippi River flowed backward.

"I'm not from this state," said the other young man. "Where I'm from, people seldom eat seafood, rolls, or fancy desserts. My people think the four major food groups are beer, hotdogs, Jell-O, and marshmallows."

"That's funny. Did you know Harry Truman, Walt Disney, and Mark Twain were all from Missouri? Our state offers more history, culture, and food variety than most people think. I hope you guys enjoy your meals," said Molly.

The two young male customers across the way fell silent, and after a trip to the kitchen and a stop at another table to settle a bill, Molly was back waitressing at our table.

"Did you guys decide what to order yet?" she asked.

"What's the fresh-fish feature for today?" Mom said.

"We have two specials, the salmon platter and the tilapia platter. Hush puppies and a crisp side salad are included with either choice."

"Salmon and tilapia never tasted that great when I tried to make them at home, but it always tastes great here," said Mom.

"That's because our fresh salmon is flown in daily from Norway and prepared with special spices on wood-fired grills. Our tilapia is flown in from Hawaii, Costa Rica, or Columbia," said Molly.

"The price for lobster at the grocery store is lower than it has been for a long time. Do you know what's driving the lower prices for lobster?" I asked.

"According to our corporate office, last year was another record year for the Maine lobster catch. The abundance is due largely to conservation measures on the part of the fisherman, along with legislation put in place a decade ago by the Bush administration," said Molly.

"It's nice to know big business and government once worked together for the good of our country," I said.

"Let me guess," said Mom. "I used to work for an obstetrician. I bet the lobster fisherman have found a way to better protect pregnant lobsters. Part of my job with the doctor was to help teach healthy practices to pregnant women."

"Female lobsters that are egg-bearing are marked on their carapace, their upper shell, and notched on their inner right flapper. Stringent practices are responsible for returning pregnant lobsters to the ocean," said Molly.

"I remember hearing about laws passed a few years ago to disallow any dragging of lobsters on the ocean floor and that they must be caught in traps," I said.

"Traps must include escape hatches for undersized lobsters, as well as biodegradable escape hatches to free lobsters in lost traps," said Molly.

"You really know your stuff, Molly," I said.

"A few of the pregnant women who came to the doctor's office were scared and probably wished they could escape," said Mom.

"It's nice to see a young woman like you beaming with confidence in such an intelligent and fun way," I said.

"Thank you so much," said Molly.

"You make your customers comfortable," said Mom.

"It's part of my job. I try to pull out all the stops to make every dining experience extra special for my customers. Because at Red Lobster, we 'sea food' differently," said Molly.

"Now you are pouring it on a little thick," said Mom.

"So what will it be: salmon, tilapia, or lobster?" asked Molly.

Mom and I ordered our food. She selected salmon and I went with the tilapia.

"Your father often mentioned that business people finalized deals over lunch or dinner," said Mom, after the waitress walked away.

"This is very true," I said. "I remember, at lunch and

dinner, Dad telling us kids to finish eating our vegetables and clean our plates. He'd say the poor children in China would love to have a full helping of cooked peas or carrots on their table at dinner time. If one of us refused to eat our food, there was no TV that night for any of us."

"That's because your father was working so hard to pay the mortgage, the car payment, and trying his best to keep food on the table for six people," said Mom.

"Dad was a good man," I said.

"Your father thoroughly enjoyed when one of his children skipped toward him when he walked into the house after a long day at work," said Mom.

"I miss that part of life now that my girls are grown," I said.

"I worry about the bills, and I worry about you as my care partner," said Mom.

"You don't think I can handle it. You don't think I'm doing a good job."

"That's not it at all. Your days are filled with balancing work, the needs of your own family, and care responsibilities. There's no doubt this juggling act takes its toll on you," said Mom.

"I try to make sure I get enough sleep," I said.

"That's why it's so important to recognize when you're stressed and to do something about it. Remember, if you don't take care of yourself, you can't possibly take care of someone else."

"I appreciate that, Mom. I will definitely try to make sure I get enough rest," I said.

"I worry too much, but I just can't help it," said Mom.

When our dinners came, Mom, a devout Catholic, bowed her head. I took my clue, and we said a short prayer together to thank the Lord for our meal.

After just one bite, Mom declared, "My salmon tastes delicious."

"My food is very good, too. Food usually tastes a little better when someone else is doing the cooking and the person doing the eating is extremely hungry," I said.

And I was hungry, not having eaten anything all day since a cup of coffee and a piece of toast early in the morning. I was happy to be enjoying a good meal and happy to see Mom enjoying her meal as well.

As I took my last bite of tilapia, Molly came by and offered us dessert.

"Not me, I'm full," said Mom.

I passed, too, and asked for the tab.

"Wait, Steve," Mom said, leaning forward and snapping her fingers. Mom always did that whenever she had an idea. "I think it would be a nice gesture if we brought back a box of breaded jumbo shrimp for Sylvia. She has been very nice to me."

"Okay, that's fine with me," I said.

"Give me time to place the order and redo the bill, and when the shrimp is ready, I'll bring it right to you. It has been a pleasure serving you," said Molly.

"The pleasure was all ours," said Mom.

"Molly, thank you for your great service," I said.

While Mom used the lady's room, I waited at the table.

When she returned ten minutes later, I decided to use the men's room, since we were still waiting for the jumbo shrimp.

When I returned to the table, Mom had her sweater around her shoulders and the white to-go box of jumbo shrimp in front of her. I stuffed two twenties and a ten-dollar bill inside the black-leather folder on the table to settle our bill, leaving Molly a nice tip.

By the time we arrived back at Bethesda, the evening shadows had lengthened and the streetlights were winking on. Mom heaved as satisfied sigh, and I could tell she had enjoyed her evening.

I reached behind my seat, grabbed Mom's cane, and handed it to her. I could have gone inside the lobby and gotten a wheelchair, but I knew Mom preferred to make the walk herself. Even though it would take a while and we must shuffle along in small increments, to her it was a matter of pride and independence. Once inside the building, we took the elevator to the second floor. Sylvia was standing in the hallway near the nurses' station.

"Did you guys enjoy your evening out?" Sylvia asked.

"Yes, we had a very nice time," said Mom, "and we brought back some carry-out for you." Mom motioned me to hand box with the shrimp to Sylvia.

"Thank you," said Sylvia, lifting the lid to see what was inside. "This had to be Audrey's idea," she said, breaking into laughter.

I didn't know what was so funny, so I peered inside. There, beside the jumbo shrimp, was Mom's half-eaten baked potato, mushy with sour cream. Apparently, when I visited the men's room just before paying our tab, Mom had slipped her potato in with the shrimp. I was a little embarrassed. I didn't know if this was a manifestation of Mom's confusion, or if she did it as a prank to play on Sylvia, since they were always teasing each other. Whatever the reason behind it, Sylvia graciously accepted Mom's odd gift, half-eaten leftovers and all.

Chapter 10

Some people draw strength and enjoyment from working in the garden, from painting, from listening to music, or from playing a musical instrument. For Mom when she was younger, a round of golf was the ticket to feeling renewed. I shared my mother's love of golf. It always gave me a chance to relax, to walk for exercise, and to think without any pressures. Whenever I was playing well, especially after shooting that rare round of par, there was immediate cause for celebration. At my age, a celebration meant a glass of cold lemonade and a hamburger at a table in the dining room of a clubhouse, with whoever played the round of golf with me.

The number of golfers playing on links courses has quadrupled since the early professional playing days of Tiger Woods and Phil Mickelson. With that development, I never played golf on weekends or holidays anymore, because golf courses are extremely crowded on those days. It's usually easier to score better when you are able to keep moving, because you can find a rhythm when you don't have to stand around waiting for other players.

The pulse and rhythm of life marked by playing golf once a week had so long ago become such an important part of Mom's world that she missed it dearly after her health declined. She had always kept her golf bag as neat as a room in a convent, her shoes cleaned and shined each morning before she went to play a round, and her outfit washed and pressed. Only the golf balls crammed into the lower pouch of her golf bag were old and dusty.

I would have loved to play one more round of golf with my parents. In their working years, my father played hundreds of rounds with my mother. Helen played hundreds of rounds with Mom in the early years of their retirement. As recently as four years ago, Mom would have loved to play golf again, but the chance that one of her pacemaker wires might work loose during a hard swing and follow-through, scared the willies out of me. I didn't want to be known as the guy who allowed his mother to die out in the open fields alone. Something like this happening, while I was looking for an errant golf ball in the woods, was unthinkable. Whenever my mother brought up the issue of me taking her out for golf, I had always found some excuse, such as, "It's too hot," "It's too cold," or "I have something else I have to do today."

My work of managing properties entails doing all sorts of things: mowing grass, mulching soil beds, landscaping, trimming bushes, painting, blowing leaves, cleaning bathrooms, stocking supplies, doing light repairs, sweeping parking lots, picking up trash, spreading salt, clearing snow, and caring for the inside and outside perimeters of buildings. Property managers focus on outside maintenance after spring storms and on dead and dying foliage during the fall before winter conditions hamper their efforts. Though much of the work is labor intensive, one good thing about my job was that usually there was flexibility in when tasks needed to be completed, as long as they were finished before days end. This allowed me the freedom to schedule work appointments around my visits to Bethesda to check on Mom, and no matter how busy things were at work, I always looked forward to my time with Mom and telephone visits with Aunt Rose.

Despite our twenty years' difference in age, Aunt Rose and I had everything in common. Somewhere beyond the pain and depression that tormented both of us, we chose an option of hope. When we talked, we discussed lower-back pain, achy knees, hemorrhoids, and colon troubles and how we were always misplacing our keys and forgetting where we put things. Then the next time we talked, I'd say, "Hey, did I tell you about my colon troubles?" and Aunt Rose would say, "No, I don't think so," and I'd tell the story of my colon problems all over again. We would add a twist to the previous way the conversation played out, making each other laugh. Then the next time we talked, we expanded our talks about our health and just about any other topic all over again. It was great.

"It's hell getting old," said Aunt Rose.

"Yeah, I know," I said.

One afternoon, on my drive to Bethesda, I noticed a giant sign that had been hung from an overpass over the highway. It said, "Save the Clowns, Impeach Obama. Honk your horn if you agree." I didn't vote for Barrack Obama in either of the elections he won, but I didn't honk as I passed under the sign, either. Though I disagreed with the majority of his administration's strategies and the general ways he tried to accomplish things, I still respected the office of the presidency.

No matter how many crazy laws are written, the fact remains, when new legislation causes victims to suffer, the victims figure that crimes were committed to pass the bill. Passing good laws requires character, intelligence, and an extremely high discernment of possible negative consequences of change. Many citizens, including some who voted for President Obama twice, were starting to believe that his administration offered only an ideology, instead of well-thought-out plans.

I recalled hearing something on the news a day or two earlier about a woman at the city manager's office in Columbia telling a couple of protestors that they had a first amendment right to make a banner and they didn't need a permit to display it. The protestors told the woman, "Our beef is not about race, Democrats, or Republicans. It is about tyranny." The 'Save the Clowns' theme was about a recent hubbub over the firing of a rodeo clown wearing a Halloween Obama mask. Rodeo clowns have been wearing masks portraying the faces of presidents for as long as there have been rodeos. But because the clown was wearing a mask portraying the face of our current black president, the gesture was portrayed as racist by the liberal media, that never seems to tell the entire story anymore.

In the name of America and the Bill of Rights, as part of a growing grassroots movement nationwide, the peaceful highway-overpass protestors had decided to take a stand in hopes of reversing the tide. They were advocating that Americans wake up to all the destructive transformation in our country and insist on investigative journalism instead of biased news reports conceived by mainstream media promoting a liberal agenda. To start the ball rolling, they thought impeaching Obama, with his own liberal agenda, would be a good move. When I walked into Mom's apartment a little while later, I found Nurse Sylvia just leaving.

"More shots," said Mom.

"I'm sure you're glad it's over," I said. "I wanted to ask you how much cash you'd like to keep in your purse. What works best for you, Mom?"

"I think twenty dollars a week is enough. I can buy the little things I need with that."

Setting up a sort of petty cash fund for incidentals was an easier matter than I had anticipated. Since I was prepared to help a little more than Mom had requested, I tried to place two twenty dollar bills in a lock box for her every week. The extra twenty allowed Mom to get her hair fixed on Fridays. Only she and I knew where we hid the small lock box in her apartment.

Mom turned away from a Tropicana orange juice commercial airing on the game channel she was watching, and, using her cane, walked over to the cupboard and grabbed two small glasses off the lower shelf. She was thirsty, but not hungry.

"I'd like mine in a glass," said Mom. "Let's have some fresh-squeezed orange juice together. There's a bag of oranges in the frig."

She walked about the kitchen cautiously, selecting a large bowl and a wire strainer that fit over the rim of the glasses. No matter her mood at the start of a day, a small glass of freshly squeezed orange juice would always lift Mom's spirits, adding some cheer and lessening the weariness of long hours of worry when she was alone.

Mom opened a cabinet above the kitchen sink; it contained a box of potato chips. Then she looked at a box of salted hard pretzels on another shelf, and finally a plastic container of Hershey candy bars in the last cabinet. Each week a candy dish magically refilled itself with Mars, Snickers, and Milky Way bars. I suspected the culprit was either my sister Karen or Mom's friend Helen, but I would never know which one, because both women were good at their trades. Karen and Helen broke the lesser rules to help those suffering have a little fun

"Where the devil is a plastic knife?" asked Mom.

She gazed with uncertainty at the cookie jar, toaster, refrigerator, and clock. A plastic knife was not in sight.

"We use plastic butter knives in the dining hall, because residents could accidentally cut themselves using sharp steak knives," said Mom.

"Sure," I said.

"Do you think the kitchen manager stores any plastic knives in her office?" asked Mom.

"Do you mean in Kim's office?" I asked.

"Yes, I was drawing a blank trying to remember her name."

"Maybe. I'll go check," I said.

I walked down the hall to the dining room and found Kim working her regular shift. From her office, between the dining room and the prep kitchen, I could hear Kim talking. As I approached closer, I saw her hair was hidden by a netted food-prep cap. She wore a white cotton button-down shirt and black loose-fitting dress pants, the kind of uniform many kitchen workers of both sexes wear to stay comfortable.

Kim's office was busy looking, in a state of organized clutter. Through a huge plate glass window, I could see a long stainless-steel table heaped with trays of sweet-smelling, fresh-baked bread and small bowls of tapioca pudding. An older woman was mixing rice and water in a cast-iron skillet. Another woman, dressed like a chef and wearing a high-reaching white hat, stood stirring sauces and vegetables in large pots.

By the politeness of the conversation from the workers surrounding Kim, I could tell she was the kind of kitchen manager who didn't hire people that didn't have good manners. It was obvious that she had no fondness for people with bad language, a dirty appearance, a bad attitude, or a propensity for showing up late for work.

"Hi Kim, how are you?" I asked.

"I'm just fine. I'm creating a new menu, mostly adding new twists to some old favorites," said Kim.

"Interesting," I said.

"I'm doing what I love, cooking for hundreds of people. What's more American than that?" said Kim.

"Nothing that I can think of right now," I said.

"And how are you?" asked Kim.

"I'm good. If a man speaks about making a change in the kitchen and there is no woman there to hear him, is he still wrong?" I asked.

"Yes, but whether a recipe starts out right or wrong, usually a minor fix can make any food on a plate look and taste fabulous," said Kim. "But if a man's personal makeup includes cussing or spitting, he is automatically disqualified from my kitchen."

"That's what I would have thought," I said.

"There are plenty of canes around here, and my associates know not to make me want to use one," said Kim. "Fortunately, nearly all of our meals are executed just fine."

"Sorry to interrupt you while you're working, but do you stock any plastic knives?"

"I warn you about all the canes that double as weapons around here, and now you want me to supply you with plastic knives to defend yourself?" asked Kim, keeping her poker face.

"Mom and I want to cut a few oranges in half," I said.

"Yes, we keep an ample supply of plastic knives in stock for those nice sunny days when we plan picnics for the residents," said Kim.

"I just need one plastic knife," I said.

Kim flung open a drawer beneath her desk. She spied a square white box and reached inside it for several small, clear plastic bags of utensils.

"Here are some plastic utensils. Your Mom can use them as needed in her apartment."

"Thank you, "I said. "Mom and I are making fresh-squeezed orange juice. Would you like me to bring you a glass?"

"I'm a coffee drinker in the morning, and it's like a ritual to start my day, but thanks anyway for thinking about me," said Kim.

"Thanks for everything you and your staff do for the residents. I've eaten a few meals here with Mom, and the food has always tasted great."

"It's my honor to cook for the elderly," said Kim. "It's what I have to give. The common denominator of all people is food, because we all have to eat."

"That's for sure. I'm just curious; do you order a lot of organic products?" I asked.

"When we can, we do. We work with local farmers and manufacturers who share our values and our commitment to environmental stewardship for the well-being of the consumer," said Kim.

"I hope more people start supporting our small local farmers," I said.

"We safeguard the environment when we move away from herbicides and pesticides, protecting the earth's soil, and helping to preserve water quality," said Kim.

"Have organic products become increasingly more popular because of all the toxins in foods?"

"Yes, but it's still hard to find cost-effective products in some categories, We try to order items that help us keep the unpronounceable ingredients out of food and off the residents' plates."

"Do you get involved with other purchases at Bethesda or just the things needed in the kitchen?"

"Mostly I order just what we need to prepare meals," answered Kim. "I did hear about an issue our purchasing people had with a manufacturer who supplied us with bottles of mouthwash."

"What happened?"

"They started watering down their product to deceive customers. You would think a company would want to keep a strong relationship with large organizations that recommend their products."

You would think the active ingredients in a large bottle of mouthwash would contain the same percentages as the small size. But when researchers hired by Bethesda tested the active ingredients, their work revealed that the percentage of sodium fluoride in the large bottles purchased from the manufacturer was half the strength of the percentages in small bottles obtained from a local dentist. I was surprised to hear that. But it made sense that any large organization with multiple locations and servicing lots of people, should pay attention to the quality and value of the things they purchased.

"Thanks for the plastic utensils. It was nice talking to you, Kim," I said.

"Nice talking to you. Have a good day!" she answered. "Don't drink too many sugary drinks or eat too much ice cream."

Kim's last comment struck me as a little odd at first. Then I realized she probably said that to everybody, in particular to the residents, trying to get them to eat a little healthier.

When I got back to the apartment, I handed Mom the packages of plastic utensils. She thanked me several times, and sliced four oranges in half. Then she squeezed the juice from the oranges and handed me a glass.

She smiled and took a sip. Over the edge of her glass, her very brown eyes sparkled at me.

"This is good stuff," she said.

"You have enough oranges left for the rest of the week," I said.

"Is that a polite way of telling me that you want to decline trying some of my orange juice?"

"No, on the contrary. I look forward to enjoying the fruits of your labor. Get it— fruits of your labor?"

"Oh, you think you're so clever," she said. "So how is your orange juice, Steve?"

"Everything wonderful, as expected."

A few evenings later when I came to visit Mom, she wasn't in her room. I walked to the activities room, and there she sat by herself, working on an enormous jigsaw puzzle. It was close to being completed.

"May I help you finish the puzzle?" I asked. "I could hand you the pieces."

"Yes, you may. So long as you promise not to touch anything," said Mom.

"Then I can't hand you the puzzle pieces, can I?" I asked, waiting for the laugh Mom usually gave when I made a joke.

"You know what I meant," said Mom, smiling but not laughing. "The idea is that residents complete their own jigsaw puzzles, so as to keep our minds working."

"I can appreciate that," I said. "Jigsaw puzzles and crosswords are fun things a person can do when alone. I'm getting to the age where doing anything with a large crowd doesn't seem special anymore."

While Mom worked at the puzzle, I looked up "jigsaw puzzle" on my laptop and learned some interesting things. The origin of jigsaw puzzles goes back to the 1760s, when John Spilsbury, an engraver and mapmaker, pasted a map onto a flat piece of wood and cut it into small pieces to help sailors learn geography. Over the centuries, jigsaw puzzles grew as educational toys, moving from lessons in geography to lessons in entertainment, helping teach about diverse subjects like nursery rhymes and animals. Probably the biggest surprise for Spilsbury would be how the elderly have embraced puzzling to help with their memory and problem-solving skills.

Jigsaw puzzles are made for every age and skill level, from four-piece puzzles for infants all the way up to thirty-two-thousand-piece puzzles. St. Louis is home to the largest jigsaw puzzle store in the world and is open to the public seven days of the week. People from across the globe visit the store in appreciation of all the diverse puzzle creations.

When Mom got tired of her puzzle, I walked with her back to her room. She settled herself slowly into her favorite chair. She seemed distant this evening, even a little irritable, which wasn't normally like her.

"The only thing I really ever wanted was that my children were prepared to become productive citizens when they reached adulthood," said Mom out of the blue.

"Hopefully something like that happened," I said.

"Well, that's an unflattering statement," snapped Mom. "You can think of something more profound than that."

"Something like that did happen," I said. "It's just that all the terror in the world makes everything seem so overwhelming sometimes, as if half the people in the world that you are going to meet are good, and half are bad."

"I'll scream if I hear you say that one more time," said Mom.

"In war and in politics, I think it's true," I said. "To pretend that all is well in America is work for a fool."

"I never believed in dwelling on negativity," said Mom. "Actually, something good is always happening. It's just that many good things never get publicized."

"You always add a considerable dimension to any argument," I answered. "I guess I'm just tired of all the crazy ideas I keep hearing about from out-of-touch politicians on the news. The wrong people are ruling our country and the world."

"Probably from questioning patients all those years when I was working, I learned what is important to people," Mom said. "Over the years my abilities improved because of my experiences raising four children. Applying what I learned from my own family structure helped me talk to young mothers in the surroundings of the doctor's office," said Mom.

"Structure is good in any setting," I said.

"If you have a wide base of knowledge to draw from to give an opinion, than you will serve others well with advice," said Mom. "Parents have to talk to their children like they are young adults, not like the young buffoons they sometimes act like when they have nothing to connect to in their background. It's also important for parents of teenagers to pick their battles."

"It's difficult for parents when their teens start ignoring them and treating them like they're stupid," I said.

"I understand that. It's like they're sticking a dagger in your back," said Mom.

"I'm glad my daughters are grown. I've learned not to get excited about the little things that are too small to worry about," I said.

"Children always want to run with the herd," said

Mom. "When they grow older and have to make important decisions, they grow out of the herd mentality."

I was hoping that this was true in the way that I had
watched my two daughters mature. And now I was trying
to motivate Mom to stay interested in making decisions,
and encouraging her to keep in touch with her close
friends.

Mom sat still in her chair, the footrest stretched out as
far as it would go. Her usually organized apartment looked
different, strange at night. Her clothes were everywhere,
on the backs of chairs, over a curtain rod in the bathroom, and strung across her bed. You could see a pile of
paperbacks on a table in the corner of the kitchen, none
of which had book markers as evidence she was reading
any of them. In her chair, Mom coughed and cleared her
throat.

"Are you okay?" I asked.

"What time is it?"

"I'm not sure, but it's getting dark outside."

"Steve, turn the light on. I'm getting tired. I'm going to
get ready for bed," said Mom. "Don't leave until I finish
changing into my pajamas. Would you change the liner in
the kitchen wastebasket and take the trash to the dumpster on your way out?"

"Sure," I said.

In her pajamas, Mom looked smaller and older than
she did in the daytime when she was dressed and wore
a little makeup. Her arms and neck looked thinner and

her hair greyer. She was too old to change her ways. She had too many health issues to do anything more challenging than just trying to exist another day. She had often reminded me about the night Dad died, lying in bed, his face blue-white and his mouth wide open, his eyes staring up at the ceiling. That night she was kneeling beside the bed holding his hands, and desperately crying, wishing there was a way for him to come alive. When I arrived to comfort Mom that evening, all she could utter is, "My poor husband, what will I do without you?" She would never fully recover, but she learned to make small adjustments over time.

When a woman loses her loving husband at an advanced stage in her life, she is told by others to take up a hobby during weekdays, go to luncheons with friends on weekends, and do something for the poor by volunteering for some cause. But Mom had difficulty adjusting to that advice because she had been doing all those things her entire life. During the first year after Dad's death, she just wanted things kept simple, so she could plan her own course of action to grieve.

After a traumatic event, feelings of abandonment stay with a person, sometimes for a decade or more. However, it was possible for Mom, after she was willing to explore the healing process, to evolve from immeasurable depths and rise to impossible heights. Even if some resentments from chapters in her life lingered, and health problems beset her, sadness and stress took a back seat to her fight for happiness. Sometimes she was her wonderful self and said funny things. Once in a while she would get in a mood, and fall silent, going around for an entire day like a stranger. Today had been one of those days.

By the time I was back from emptying the trash and finished placing a fresh liner in the wastebasket, Mom was already under the covers resting comfortably.

"Okay, Mom. I'll visit you again in a few days," I said.

"Okay, honey," said Mom. "I'll talk to you later."

"Sleep good," I said.

I kissed her on the cheek. It wasn't a very cold night, but her face felt chilled just the same. In her bedroom, the window didn't fit tightly, and wind slithered into the room. But with all her extra blankets, her bed was still warm, so she snuggled up in it, pulled the covers over her left ear and around her face like a hood. The nurses, when they needed to do something, and her friend Helen when she visited, always insisted Mom wake up when she was sound asleep. Though nobody ever said anything about it, everyone was afraid of being the person who had to wake her, afraid of what they might find, afraid she might not move. As I left the bedroom, I noticed Mom's breathing sounded shallower than usual. I remembered Nurse Sylvia mentioning that Mom had slept many more hours than usual over the past four days.

When I walked into my own house, the phone was ringing. I picked it up, and a woman on the other end asked if I would be willing to answer a few questions about my views regarding freedom in education. Earlier in the day, President Obama honored sixteen men and women as Presidential Medal of Freedom recipients, none of whom were Caucasian males.

"Do you have five minutes to take a survey for a good cause?" asked the female telemarketer.

"I normally don't give out information over the phone, but I will help you tonight," I said.

"What year were you born?"

"I was born in 1954," I said.

"Is anyone in the household under fifty-years-old and home right now?" said the voice.

"No," I said.

"Sorry, I've asked you all the qualifying questions I'm allowed at this point. We have a lesser quota for the number of men in your age group in our survey."

It was ironic. The one time I offered to help with a survey over the phone, I was rejected. For some time there has been a major shift in how everything works. The average working Caucasian man over fifty is being told he is too old and too backward for modern society, that his capitalistic ways are wrong for progress. But the day will come when the people spreading this philosophy will find out how wrong they were to think that way. When the efforts and the money of this sector of men dries up, there will be very few men left with enough expertise in managing grand plans to pay for all the government programs.

God knows that by the time a man is fifty, he should know that no man is invincible. Why do people even believe that they need politicians, especially inexperienced ones, to enlighten them about the pitfalls of life? Just thinking about all the men who think they can hoot with the owls at night, and then soar with the eagles the next day, made me realize that most men are pitiful creatures. They are bound for a common fate, much like animal species.

Animals are always showing us their tactics of survival, proving the skills they are good at and the talents they lack in the wild. Opossums are small, tree-dwelling mammals smart enough to carry and protect their young in their pouches. But because their eyesight is bad and they are easily stimulated and preoccupied when seeing road kill or food that has fallen from trees, they may run out in the street in front of a speeding car to investigate. A deer will run away from danger when spooked by loud noises, but will freeze and stare back when distracted by the headlights of an oncoming car. Squirrels travel from tree to tree like world-class trapeze acrobats, but they have no understanding of electrical charges that flow through the wires installed by public utility companies. As soon as they encounter a hot current, they fall to their death, when all they were doing was trying to follow an easier path to where they were going.

Maybe humans are more like animals than we care to admit. Men and women fill their days with work, exercise, preparing meals, and safely going about their business in hopes of getting ahead. Then when they sit behind the wheel of their car, they talk and text on their cell phones. Sitting in the driver's seat and steering a car along the narrow lanes of an interstate is the one place on Earth that people should use the highest amount of caution. Yet drivers choose not to set aside their cell phones, when they know they should hold off on social media until they get to their destination. Decisions like that are no smarter than some of the ones made by animals living out in the wild.

Chapter 11

On my next visit to see Mom, the grass in yards was fully green and the trees were abounding with blooms. Mom was sitting underneath the overhang of the patio outside her apartment, eagerly awaiting me, and sitting on a concrete bench with her cane at her side.

"How are you, Mom?" I asked.

"Pretty good, I like this warmer weather, but it's still a little chilly in the shade," she said. "I've lived here for four and a half months now, and I thought it looked like a good day to sit outside."

"The beautiful garden here is starting to bloom," I said.

Silence begged an answer, but Mom said nothing. Finally she spoke.

"The first few months here at Bethesda was fun, because everything was new. But I'm just worried that everything has turned routine. My life is already curtained off. If all I do is dress, eat, undress, and sleep, my life is like traveling in a train at night, going on and on in the darkness, without a chance to enjoy the view," said Mom.

"Well, it's still three weeks before the swimming pools

open. That's when summer is officially here," I said. "Though some people say it's when the Cubs come to town for their second road series of the season with the Cardinals. Our days will liven when the Cubs come to town."

"Let's go back inside and talk," said Mom.

When Mom was using her cane, she kept her wheelchair parked in the corner of her living room, next to the TV. When we got to her apartment, I sat down on the sofa and I noticed her stuffed toy bear sitting on her wheelchair. That bear had a history. Three years before he died, Dad, along with Mom, volunteered to work in a booth at the Affton Days Festival to help raise money for charity. The game at their booth required a player to toss two of three washers into a quart-sized tin can from ten feet away to win a prize. Winners had a choice of a stuffed animal or a pick from several framed pictures of St. Louis sports celebrities Kurt Warner, Marshall Faulk, Ozzie Smith, Brett Hull, Hale Irwin, and Mark McGwire. The stuffed animals were donated by a toy company located in Herman, Missouri. The framed photos were donated by a local sporting good store. One little boy paying the cost of one dollar per try, failed to toss two washers into the tin can during any of his attempts. After he spent ten dollars, Mom gave the little boy his choice of picking a prize anyway. He loved baseball, so he was thrilled when Mom allowed him to grab a framed picture of his hero, Mark McGwire. Any type of sports memorabilia featuring Mark McGwire was a hot find back then for any boy who loved baseball, until leaks of steroid use linked the hero with other abusers being accused of rocking the baseball world.

By the time the festival shut down that evening, all the stuffed animals and framed photos had been won and given away as prizes, except for one fussy, brown stuffed bear that was missing a nose. Mom offered the stuffed bear to a few fairgoers and to all her grandchildren when she next saw them, but there were no takers. So she kept the bear for herself. She decided to sew on a special black button to repair its nose. She brushed the fur, but then decided to go one step further and took the bear to a dry-cleaner. When she picked it up two days later, it had a new look and a fresh clean-linen smell. She placed the stuffed bear between the pillows on her bed. When she went to sleep that first night with the refurbished plush toy next to her, she rolled over on it, and the bear talked, waking her. It was then that Mom realized her stuffed bear held a recording device inside, and by squeezing its right paw once, a person could play a message. By squeezing twice, a new message could be recorded over an old message.

As I sat in Mom's Bethesda apartment staring at her bear in the wheelchair, she walked up and squeezed its paw.

"The bear has something it wants to say to you," she muttered.

"Thank you for helping me, Steve," said the recording of Mom's voice, the first and simplest message she recorded specifically for me.

"Sure Mom," I said. "No worries. I wouldn't have it any other way."

This was a touching display of affection, but it was only a prelude to what awaited the nurses, other residents, and visitors at Bethesda. No one can say exactly how many messages Mom recorded, but it was a lot. My estimate put the number at between eight and twelve every day during the first half of that summer. It may have been the most messages ever recorded anywhere to specifically pay tribute to and elderly people.

During the time when Congress was in session and the Democrats and Republicans were finding it impossible to agree on a military budget, or any budget for that matter, Mom recorded the following message, the longest message I heard from her bear: "Dear Mr. President, all the political favors to people who voted for you, but your administration can't invite all the surviving World War II veterans in advance of the opening of their newly built memorial. Those brave men fought for our country."

There seems to be a myth that brave people never fear death. It's what people do to overcome fear that makes them brave. They push limits, accept their physical disabilities, and are able to harness the powers of their conscious minds to go beyond the expectations of others, against immense odds. Real people believe deeply in what they are doing. Whether it's fighting to help someone else or battling a disease, they do their best to prevail over anything that is trying to take them down. Watching my Mom develop a system of mental domination to thwart all the symptoms of her diseases almost made me break down and cry on a number of occasions. But my strong manly side kept my emotions in check so as not to create unnecessary tension that might inflict more distress on Mom.

When her lady resident friend Virginia wasn't feeling good one day, Mom recorded these words on the recorder inside her stuffed bear: "Feel better soon Virginia, and its nice to have you as my friend." Probably just a coincidence, but Virginia started feeling much better the next day. When Helen came to visit on a rainy day, Mom recorded a message for her friend and former golfing partner: "I guess a round of golf is out of the question today."

Usually when I visited now, Mom stayed awake for maybe two hours before she needed to lie back down and rest. That was the routine on this day, both of our lives filled with our certain habits to make things work. In bed and still wearing sweat clothes, Mom closed her eyes, rolled over, and went to sleep. A few minutes later, leaning across to the other side of the bed, she whispered, "George, are you awake?" There was no answer, and after a moment, she rolled over again, this time falling sounder asleep. There wasn't any further talking, just intermittent bouts of light snoring.

After Dad died and Mom was still living in her house, she said she often heard him talking to her or asking for something. She said the sounds never frightened her and that she would listen for a while, and then they would go away.

An hour later and still at her apartment, as I was watching "The Five" on the Fox channel, Mom started talking in her sleep again, "When I was in prison," she said.

"Mom, what are you talking about?" I asked, my voice causing her to open her eyes.

"Your Dad came to visit me and talked to me through the steel bars," she said.

"Mom, your talk is starting to creep me out," I said.

She listened for a moment and then looked at me as if disappointed that I had reminded her of reality. Soon enough, she was fully awake. She took her time to dress, brush her hair, and streak a light shade of lipstick on her lips. I walked with her slowly to the dining room. Her shoulders were hunched, as if to signal a decreasing desire to keep moving forward, wishing she could go back twenty years to when she was with her husband and both of them were healthy. She wished she could walk right past the nurses' station without being stopped for any reason, without needing shots or medicine.

Mom still loved getting her hair fixed, so after eating dinner together—a meal consisting of baked chicken, spaghetti, mashed potatoes, peas, and cornbread—I escorted her to Bethesda's in-house beauty salon for the beautician's first appointment of the evening. We only had to wait about five minutes for the hairstylist to arrive, and when she did, Mom gave her a mischievous grin.

"Make me look like Jamie Lee Curtis or Jacqueline Kennedy," said Mom. "It's been many years since I was young and beautiful."

"You are wrong about that last part," said the hairstylist. "You still have great hair and beautiful eyes. I like your dimples when you smile, too."

"Thank you," said Mom.

"From what the nurses and some of the other residents say, you are a wonderful woman, said the stylist. "What they say is enough to keep you beautiful forever."

"You are very kind," said Mom.

"Your hair is a bit longer than Jamie Lee Curtis's. Let's go with a Jacqueline Kennedy look. I can shape your hair on the sides of your face and in the back with waves like she had. As you probably already know, when John F. Kennedy was president, many people admired him, but I think just as many people admired his wife," said the stylist.

"I loved both of them," said Mom.

"What was he like?" asked the hairstylist.

"President Kennedy had business savvy that he learned from his father. He had the support of his brother, Bobby, who was always in the room, and he stayed in constant contact with senators and generals when he delegated authority."

"You liked the way he governed?" questioned the hairstylist.

"For the most part, because he was much better than President Obama at checking with people to make sure his plans were right and running smoothly. I was in the kitchen listening to the radio when I heard that Kennedy had been shot. I immediately began sobbing," said Mom.

"Surely, the news shook emotions in people all over the world," said the stylist.

"The principal at my children's school announced it over the intercom and ordered the bus company to have their drivers take all the students home to watch the proceedings on television. In a short period of time, we learned about a man named Lee Harvey Oswald, a far-left extremist, the person who pulled the trigger."

"His assassination was such a meaningless act," said the stylist.

"President Kennedy had such a command of the English language," said Mom.

"We will never know what he may have been able to accomplish in eight years."

"President Obama is also a gifted speaker," said the stylist.

Mom shifted in her chair. "President Obama received a Nobel Peace Prize for winning a campaign, before ever doing anything as president, anything to help the cause of peace," said Mom. "He was portrayed by the media as this great man, but he had really had done very little governing in his political career before announcing his run for the presidency. Because of power of social media, and the lightning speed at which messages could be sent, young voters bought all the hype. Believe me, there's all the difference in the world between Obama and John F. Kennedy."

I kept my mouth shut, but my mind raced with thoughts about what was actually occurring in America and the far-reaching strategies I believed were badly influencing the direction of the country I love. Vote for me. Everybody else hates you. I have your back. Before you go to bed tonight, think about all I will do for you to make your life better. Vote for me, because there is a war against you. I will take care of you. Women, there is a war against you. The world hates women. Because you are a poor innocent female, I will make sure you get free contraceptives and higher pay. Black men, there is a war against you. Cops are murdering all the good black men. Stay home, I will send you free food and free healthcare. Mexican people, there is a war against you. Forget about fixing anything in your country, just get across the border, vote for me, and I will take care of you. Indians, there is a war against you. Washington and the NFL hate you and want to deface your name. College students, there is a war against you. When you graduate, you should instantly own a four-bedroom house with a three-car garage, a fenced yard, and a roof with the fanciest shingles known to man. Pick whichever neighborhood you want to live in, and I will help you. Vote for me. Eighteen-year-olds, there is a war against you. You should make three times the minimum wage. You are under great pressure, and small businesses and big corporations are bungling your future by taking advantage of you. But forget your worries; I'll take care of you. Vote for me. For a life devoted to loveliness. Vote for me America. Canned beets, there is a war against you. I wish you could vote. I would make sure to prolong your existence in a tin can, and then when prices went higher, I would devour you.

"President Obama has three more years of his second term to carry out his agenda," said the hairstylist. "I think it's too soon to judge him."

"Obama is a young president. His smartest move was knowing how to connect with young people using social media. The other older candidates read newspapers and talked to people at town meetings, but they underestimated the power of social media," said Mom.

"What did Kennedy do to enhance his chances of winning the presidency?" asked the hairstylist.

"You mean, besides his charm and good looks?" asked Mom.

"Yes, what did he say and do to get people to like him?"

"He was our first modern president helped by the advances of television. He spoke to moderate Democrats and Republicans. He was a devout Catholic, who spoke to pro-life believers and other Christians. Women too scared to deal with a pregnancy were having back-alley abortions back then. He spread hope to single mothers and families," said Mom.

"Did he promise to improve the economy?" asked the stylist.

"He promised to lower taxes, and he did, but it was something Democrats had never done in previous administrations."

"I think I probably would have voted for Kennedy back then if I would have had the chance," the stylist murmured.

"Just remember, don't buy into any of that stuff when the politicians tell you we must pass a bill to find out what is in it, like Speaker Nancy Pelosi tried to tell the public in hopes of influencing our thinking about the Affordable Care Act," said Mom.

"What do you remember most about the 60's and 70's?" asked the stylist.

"Lyndon Johnson was forced into duty as president when Kennedy was assassinated. The war in Vietnam confused everyone at home, but U. S. soldiers knew as soon as they stepped foot in the jungle that there was no solid plan for the way to fight. The Beatles were changing the music scene," said Mom.

"What do you remember about the Beatles?" asked the hairstylist.

"I'm not sure if they picked their name after the insects," said Mom. "Their haircuts made them look a little like the insects. Their careers took flight after just one appearance on the Ed Sullivan Show. Young women would scream and pass out, unable to control their emotions while listening to them perform. I think timing had a lot to do with their success. The world needed a diversion away from all its problems. While music lovers were listening to songs from the Beatles, riots broke out in the streets after Dr. Martin Luther King was assassinated."

"What do you remember about him?" asked the stylist.

"He grappled with the war in Vietnam," said Mom.

"He was against the war?"

"His issue was different than that. He believed it was wrong that the U. S. government was sending a disproportionate number of black soldiers, whose standards were compromised at home, to fight and die in hopes of raising standards in a foreign land, when we hadn't yet solved our own civil rights issues."

"How did young blacks react to King's non-violence message?" asked the stylist.

"Young 'black power' activists and organizers were calling non-violence obsolete. Dr. King understood their anger, but he continued on, steadfast in his beliefs about taking on the establishment to clarify civil rights issues in America in peaceful ways," said Mom. "One of Dr. King's main goals was to pass the civil rights bill. Many people don't realize that legislation was led by a bi-partisan Republican charge in Congress," said Mom. "Not a single Republican voted yes to pass Obama's Affordable Care Act."

I didn't join the conversation at this point because both women were doing fine without me. Besides, I was enjoying just sitting there and listening to their comments about our nation's history. Their words sparked a memory inside me. In a speech, Dr. Martin Luther King, Jr. said, "I have a dream that one day every valley shall be exalted, every hill and mountain shall be made low, the rough places will be made plain, and the crooked places will be made straight, and the glory of the Lord shall be revealed and all flesh shall see it together. The marvelous new militancy which has engulfed the Negro community must not lead us to distrust of all white people." It was part of his speech that I memorized in high school.

I always enjoyed talking about politics, but I preferred not to push any conversation, to the point where a serious argument might result while I was visiting Bethesda. The residents and the employees had enough to focus on with their daily challenges.

The hairstylist was finished, so Mom thanked and paid her, and we started back down the hall. Mom's vocalized urge to use the bathroom triggered a thought in both of our brains that we wished she could quicken her pace, but she just couldn't bend or move fast anymore. Finally we reached the entrance to her apartment, she turned the lock, flung open the door, dropped her keys on the floor, handed me her cane, and shuffled as fast as she could into the bathroom. Observing her efforts was like watching a tall woman in stilettos try to get into a Volkswagen Beetle parked on an icy street.

I waited in the kitchen. I worried about the subtle changes I seemed to be seeing in Mom. Sometimes her mind was as sharp as ever, especially when she reminisced about times past, as she had done with the hairstylist. But at other times, it seemed her mind was fading. She seemed to becoming more tired by the week. I wondered how much time in this world Mom truly had left.

"Dr. Carey, you can tell me if I'm going to die soon," I recalled Mom saying to her cardiologist some weeks back. "I'm not afraid to die."

"Audrey, I can't tell you when you are going to die. Only God knows when each of us is going to die," Dr. Carey had answered.

"I'm not afraid to die," muttered Mom, repeating herself.

"I can tell you that I will keep working with you to find the best alternatives for you to maintain a quality of life and moderate any pain you experience," said Dr. Carey.

Mom's wishes were that she not have CPR under any circumstances, and she kept a do-not-resuscitate card placard under a magnet on her refrigerator. Also on her refrigerator this day was a hand-written note to herself. It read: "Return Helen's call. Ask Steve if grass is getting cut at house. Have him spray something on weeds in back yard and check if there's mail in mailbox." She wrote down everything about the present, otherwise there was a good chance she would forget, with her questions and thoughts seldom returning. Though her memory about things that happened a long time ago was still surprisingly sharp, she increasingly described more recent events in a confusing and blurry fashion.

"There's a new lady moving in down the hall," Mom had told me one day some weeks back. "There's something different about her."

"Oh, like what?" I asked.

"Her hair is the color of rust, a squeaky sound comes out of her voice-box when she coughs, and her body parts move slow," said Mom.

"The way you are describing her, it sounds like her bearings need a good oil lube," I said.

"She's here for rehabilitation, not oil lubrication. I think she is only here for a temporary stay."

Mom never mentioned the woman again. I never met the lady, either. There was a chance the woman did a stint of rehab and moved back home, but more likely she was just part of a story that was mostly fictitious. I found it hard to believe the nurses would place a rehab patient in the same wing with the assisted living residents. I was pretty sure Mom's report came from being confused.

"Steve, I need your help," Mom called from the bathroom.

"Okay," I said, hurrying to spring from the chair where I was sitting.

"Please find some toilet paper for me; there's none left on the roll in here," Mom yelled. "I can't bend down to look in the cabinet drawers. Maybe there's another roll in the closet."

"No, none in the cabinet drawers," I said after looking.

"Oh, boy," said Mom.

"There's none in the closet either."

"Find Mable, the lady who stocks supplies, or find Sylvia. They can help you find some toilet paper."

As I was about to enter the hallway to look for help, the fire alarm sounded. I could see nurses Sylvia and Iesha scrambling at the other end of the hall and starting to wheel residents out of the building.

"What's going on?" hollered Mom, still sitting on the toilet.

"I'm not sure," I said. "It looks like either there's a fire, or Bethesda is running a fire drill. The nurses are wheeling people out."

"Steve, I need help. Do something," Mom said, starting to cry.

"Okay, hold on," I said.

"Oh, boy. Diarrhea is running down my leg. Hurry up, please," Mom called, now in a panic.

Raw emotions hit me like a ton of bricks. Don't panic and do something, I told myself. Think like a problem solver and come up with a solution, and do it quickly. It was bad timing for a fire drill, but there's never a good time for a building ablaze. Where was Aunt Rose when I needed her? Where was Kathy or Karen or Patti? There was no time to feel sorry for myself. Mom needed help immediately.

No toilet paper was in sight. No staff were in sight. All I could spot was a piece of coarse sandpaper left behind by a maintenance worker from making a repair, and two stacks of books pushed up against each other on a table. But ripping the pages out of books went against my most basic principles.

I hurried into Mom's kitchen and located a large, thick oven mitt from a cabinet drawer, the kind Mom used for taking warm items out of the microwave. I grabbed several squares from a paper towel roll hanging from a spindle on the wall. Then I hurried into the bathroom, helped Mom stand, folded the paper towel squares into the oven mitt on my right hand, and after moving close to target the area of the back of her leg that needed cleaning, I closed my eyes, ready to start wiping. No other person must ever know what I was about to do for my Mom.

I was used to the pain of seeing the subtle signs of Mom's suffering—the slightly deeper breaths she took, the soundless ways she glanced at things with her eyes, and the slow painful reaches she endured to lift a spoon or fork as she fed herself were hurtful to watch. But this event in the bathroom was as agonizing as anything I had previously witnessed or was called upon to do to help provide assistance for my mother.

"What's the oven mitt for?" said Nurse Sylvia, walking in through the bathroom doorway at just the critical moment.

"Don't ask. Thank God you are here," I said.

"We need to work fast. The fire department never tells us when we are going to have a fire drill. Have the wheelchair ready outside the door, and I'll finish up in here," said Sylvia. "Wait for us, and you can wheel your Mom outside."

Moments later, the bathroom door opened, and Mom was ready to go. While she held onto the wall rail, I put the wheelchair close to the back of her legs, and she sat down. I pushed her down the hall to the nearest elevator, while Sylvia checked to see if any other residents needed assistance in joining the roundup outside.

There were three exits on the first floor that all led, via sidewalks, to the area where we needed to go to meet the others who were already outside. We used the exit opposite the rear lobby at the end of the hall. Exiting that way, I had to maneuver the wheelchair down two steps and onto a sidewalk that sloped up a hill and wrapped around the building to the area where we were to assemble. We probably could have utilized a shipping elevator to escape, but because I was not sure if it was a shortcut, it was a risky route, and I passed on it.

At Bethesda, the safety of residents and employees is taken very seriously, which is why they collaborate with local first responders to participate in mock disaster drills. The police department, fire department, and the community emergency response team joined the Bethesda staff to conduct the mock evacuation efforts. The mock drill was planned as if a fire, common occurrences in the Midwest after major storms or tornados, caused damage to multiple campus buildings and an explosion in the main kitchen. The exercise began as a tornado watch, but then escalated into a warning, and eventually the staff began moving residents down the hallway and outside through the nearest exits after make-believing damage and fire were spotted. Per the appropriate protocol, fire trucks, ambulances, and incident command vehicles began arriving at Bethesda. They treated the drill as a real emergency, with firefighters connecting hoses and teams conveying their emergency supplies into the buildings to assess the situation for rescue.

Soon Mom and I joined the other residents, mostly in wheelchairs, and the employees, all standing on the sidewalk in front of the main entrance. A minute or two later, Sylvia joined us.

"We've weathered the perfect storm," I said. "Like the final stage of a hurricane when the swirling clouds and moisture fall to sea level, rotate around, and force more air into the eye, gaining speed and strength until the storm moves over land, while disrupted people travel in an opposite direction."

"Let's not get carried away," said Mom.

"You are funny, Steve," said Sylvia. "Bran is the plan. If we can get your Mom to start her day with that in mind, the rest will follow. Bran flakes are full of fiber and they can help hold a day together," said Sylvia.

"Don't encourage him," said Mom.

"Sylvia, you have a good sense of humor, too," I said.

The firemen had finished checking the terraces, parlors, restrooms, meeting rooms, and all the apartments. The library, dining hall, and all exits in and out of the building were cleared. While all the residents and employees were gathered together for post-drill evaluation, the fire chief gave the all clear and addressed his audience.

"Although there are a few things we can improve upon, we are pleased with most of the results of the drill, and the measures used to quickly evacuate people from the building," said the fire chief. "We look forward to putting what we learned in this mock drill today into any evacuation plan we may need in the future."

Standing near me, Sylvia glanced up at the grey sky. I followed her lead and looked up at the sky, too. The light drizzle that had been coming down was little more than a summer mist, and in the west was a giant opening in the clouds, announcing that sunlight was about to dominate the skyline.

Chapter 12

loved Bethesda because the people who worked there were good and honest. Scandals were non-existent there. People there told the truth and never worried about covering their lies. Unexpectedly, Bethesda was changing the shape of my social life, filling it with new challenges in new circumstances that I found fascinating to explore. This place was now part of me—a neighborhood of goodness, a second home, a world where I was comfortable being myself. The considerateness of the staff extended not just to the residents but to their families. Sometimes one of the nurses would gently say to me, "You look tired; you should go home and get some sleep."

It's interesting how our social life changes over the years. In our late teens, our friends are people we grew up with and either found trouble with or stayed clear of trouble with for the most part. In our twenties and thirties we still have many friends, but mostly we only have time for our children and our work, trying to grow a career. In our forties, when we're more established, we spend more time with business associates. In our fifties and early sixties, we spend more time thinking about and trying to prepare for retirement, and probably caring for elderly parents or relatives. If we are fortunate to live into our seventies or eighties, we may start searching for new friends who help to fill the large void created by the death of loved ones, in hopes we might rekindle the sort of fond and trusting relationships we remember from youth.

Evening again, and still I am here at Bethesda. The late sun was beginning to sink below the horizon, and I should have been concerned about going home to read my mail, check my messages from work, or maybe just take a nap. My mail had been piling up for days. Keeping up with all the bills, advertisements, letters, invoices for my business, and unsolicited mail every day was a battle hard to stay current with and win. As we sat together in the twilight, Mom began to speak on one of her favorite topics.

"I don't know how we allowed all this to happen to our country," said Mom. "You know I love baseball, and I don't mean to be picking on sports fans, but citizens need to start showing as much interest in our history as in what team wins on Saturday or Sunday,"

"Not enough of our citizens are paying attention to what is really happening in government," I said.

"That's what I mean," said Mom. "When a person knows more about history and politics, they make better decisions at the voting booth."

"What did you think of Bud Seiling, the commissioner of baseball?" I asked. "Some people thought he avoided hot topics and was slow to act."

"On the contrary," said Mom. "Now there was a man who knows how to fix things. He showed patience and courage, without rushing in to change everything at the risk of messing up the things that worked."

"Maybe you're right," I said.

"Cheating politicians, cheating baseball players, and cheating businessmen never seem to learn that dishonesty always bites you in the butt and comes back to haunt you. It's always a bad idea to deceive the public," said Mom.

"So what do you think the commissioner accomplished?" I asked.

"Do you remember when he stood up and told the players association that he represented the good guys, not the cheaters?" asked Mom.

"I remember something like that."

"The commissioner put a stop to steroid abuse and brought drug testing to the game despite resistance and without receiving praise from anyone," said Mom. "The media slammed him for interfering with the game, but he put an end to a lot of the cheating in baseball."

"I liked when he started inner-league play and added the wild-card teams to the playoff picture to increase interest and hope for more fans," I said.

"He led the charge to build baseball fields in inner cities to bring more interest to boys who were only playing basketball and football," said Mom. "We need more American boys playing the game, like they did in the old days."

"You make a valid point," I said. "Baseball, hotdogs, and apple pie once ruled American culture."

"Maybe we should replace hotdogs with something healthier, but I think if people paid more attention to the real issues surrounding baseball, working toward making things better, instead of only caring about what player has the most homeruns or what pitcher has the most wins, they would make better decisions in their own lives," said Mom.

"With so many cell phones in use today, too many young people aren't taking the time to sit down to read newspapers and books either," I said. "They only read the headlines of texts and only pay attention to who is at the top of the charts."

"They are denying their brains the real opportunities to learn the full story about subjects," said Mom. "Texting is rigid and narrow and just a way to follow the herd."

"Books were written a long time ago warning that Americans would have to sacrifice more because of increasing national debt," I said.

"But liberal politicians don't worry about debt, and authentic conservative politicians are becoming an endangered species," said Mom. "When people believe everything should get handed to them for free, instead of bettering their skills to earn what they want, solutions become increasingly harder to wrangle. Every person who has had their butt kicked by life, and is trying to do the right thing, deserves an opportunity. Only a lazy person is satisfied with handouts," said Mom.

Mom sat musing silently a few moments. "We have a big need, too, for clearing out the massive amounts of illegal drugs infiltrating our neighborhoods," she said finally. "As far as I am concerned, the state legislators in Colorado and Washington are wrong in considering the legalization of marijuana. We already have enough people in the U. S. walking around with unclear minds Legalizing marijuana is just making it a bigger problem than it already is now in our neighborhoods, as if the police need another vice to manage, besides illegal guns, alcohol, and heroin."

"It's as if we are sending a signal to children that drug use is a socially acceptable way of behavior in America," I said.

"What is happening to the American Dream?" asked Mom.

"Do you think you experienced most of the dreams you had as a young girl in your lifetime?" I asked.

"Well, I had intended to go to medical school. When I finished high school, St. Louis University offered me a full academic scholarship, but my father was dying from cancer and I needed to work so I could help my mother pay the bills," said Mom.

"Then you met Dad, and everything started changing again."

"Your father was the love of my life. After I met him, my plans and focus changed. Having four children brought us joy and kept us concentrating on the things that mattered. I was fortunate to work for two doctors, who fulfilled my desire to work in a field where I truly helped people," said Mom, with a mixture of pride and defiance in her voice.

No matter how intelligent and informed she was, no

matter how refined and good she was as a person, Mom was having difficulty disguising her hurt and tears about the direction the politicians were taking our country. She could call off the entire conversation with me, and I would understand.

"I was fortunate to have you and Dad as my parents," I said.

"We tried to be good parents," said Mom.

"I tried to teach my daughters some of the same things you and Dad taught me," I said. "Dad told me he walked ten miles to school in the snow when he was a boy."

"Did you believe him?" asked Mom.

"Not really. I don't think I ever did. Trying to act like the typical father, when Amanda started kindergarten, I tried to tell her that I walked five miles to school in the rain. I cut the distance in half and substituted rain in place of snow to make the story more believable. Not buying it, she asked, 'Why? Couldn't you find your bus stop?' That was my Amanda—always inquisitive, too smart for her own britches," I said.

Mom laughed. "She takes after me. She's smart, like her grandmother."

"When raising daughters, you have to act like you are smart, even when you're confused," I said.

"Both your daughters have always known that you love them," said Mom.

"I just wanted each of my girls to absorb their surroundings, and instead of always taking things, offer something in return to earn their way," I said. "I wanted them to understand more about life, to grab as much maturity and wisdom as they could as they had their life experiences."

"I think you were the kind of father who was opposed to his daughters staying too long in babyhood."

"I wanted my daughters to learn enough, so they were prepared for what's ahead. I wanted them to act smart and polite, and responsive to matters that are important."

"Even during times when they saw you raising your voice and losing your temper with them?" asked Mom.

"I know I made some mistakes," I said.

"Losing your temper is like throwing rocks at a polar bear. It's a stupid thing to do if you want to quell a situation," said Mom.

"Going overboard is wrong, but when I think back to my school days, the teachers who were hardest on their students were often the ones who cared most about them."

"I agree that children have to learn when to speak and when to listen," said Mom. "But good parenting has to include listening and staying in control, too."

"I think we learn when we get older, that good parenting, good business, and good politics have to include a good amount of listening to the plans that are formulated," I said.

"And after children grow up, they should never be too busy to make a two-minute phone call to check on their mother," said Mom.

"Baseball was always my favorite sport," I said, purposely changing the direction of the conversation.

"You were always telling your father and me that you

were going to replace Tim McCarver as the catcher for the St. Louis Cardinals. When you signed your first major league contract, you would buy us a bigger house and we could retire," said Mom with a smile.

"I guess that plan ended for me sometime during my high school years, when I realized how many other good athletes played baseball at an elite level."

"All you wanted to do was play sports, especially baseball. You were constantly asking your father to play catch with you in the backyard," said Mom.

In four or five instances, when my neighborhood friends and I were playing baseball in the backyard, someone aimed badly and broke the basement window at the back of the house. Dad never confiscated the ball or got angry about the damage. He only got better and faster at installing the new glass every time he had to fix the window. Maybe in the way he reacted to trivial things, he was teaching me to move out of my self-absorption, the malady that afflicts most children before they mature. Sometimes it takes a long time for certain children to grow up, although the crisis of a serious family illness can speed up that process at any age.

"We quit playing catch when Dad hurt his wrist. Remember? He was sitting in a lawn chair at a work picnic, and all of the sudden it collapsed to the ground when a drunken stranger bumped into him," I said.

"Your father's radius bone popped through the skin, doing nerve damage to his right hand," said Mom. "He would never regain the feeling in it."

"I remember one Saturday morning when your father grabbed the skillet from the top of the stove thinking he would wipe it clean and make pancakes. Because he had no feeling in his hand, he couldn't tell the skillet was hot and that someone had already cooked in it. Though he couldn't feel it, the entire palm of his hand swelled to one big, ugly blister," said Mom.

"During our lifetimes, we endure enough aches and pains," I said.

"But usually not as many when we are young. It isn't fun getting old," said Mom.

"When I was young, we had no childproof lids on medicine bottles, and when my friends and I rode our bikes, we had no helmets, not to mention the risks my friends and I took hitchhiking," I said. "When we rode bikes to a friend's house, there was no need to knock on the door or ring the bell more than once, because we would just walk in and announce ourselves. Or we'd sing out our friends' names to see if they could come out and play."

"Cars were without seatbelts when you were a child," said Mom.

"My friends and I drank water from the garden hose, and if any one of us had a soft drink, we shared the can," I said. "No one in the neighborhood ever died from either of those practices."

"I baked bread and cupcakes, using white flour and real butter, and made Kool-Aid with plenty of sugar for you and your friends when you played outside in the backyard," said Mom. "There were no warnings directed at mothers about the dangers of eating too much sugar or butter."

"Boys would leave their houses early in the morning and stay outside all day. Mother's didn't worry about their sons as long as they were back for supper," I said.

"Times are different," said Mom. "I remember all four of you kids running barefoot in the backyard, and using my good glass canning jars trying to catch lightning bugs."

"In the good old days, before cell phones and social networks, children figured out where their friends were congregating by looking to see which house or ball field had a pile of bicycles piled up in the driveway or on the grass," I said.

"Things that were once an adventure became monotonous and routine," said Mom.

I said nothing to that. Instead, as I watched my mother's eyes starting to slowly close, I kissed her on the forehead and drew a wool blanket from an upper shelf in the closet, covering her torso and legs. She allowed herself to drift off to sleep. I left and walked down the hall, waving goodnight to the nurses who were readying nightly medications for the residents.

Chapter 13

Three days later, Mom took a turn for the worse. Tests revealed evidence of a leaky heart valve and possible internal bleeding in a weakened wall of her small intestinal tract. The doctors said it was time to call the family. Mom was dying, but how long she would last—weeks? days?—no one could predict. Her long fight was finally almost over. The doctors said there was no more they could do. Mom was moved to Bethesda's hospice unit.

I drove to the airport to pick up Aunt Rose. After parking my truck on the yellow level at the airport garage, I walked down three flights of steps and through a tunnel to get inside to the baggage claim area for arriving passengers. Summer travelers jockeyed for position at the carousel. Aunt Rose appeared, approaching from Concourse-B, wearing a sky-blue outfit with tiny tucks all over it. She always looked beautiful because her tastes in clothes were classy and sophisticated. She knew how to shop to achieve her look without breaking the bank.

"Good morning, Aunt Rose," I said, hugging her. I'd met her right on time, and as we approached the baggage claim area, her suitcases were shooting out the opening at the top of the luggage conveyor.

"Good morning, honey," she answered.

Not that long ago, before cell phones were invented, visitors could show up early at the airport, walk down to a terminal, and wait for a friend or relative arriving from another city. Watching airplanes take off and land while enjoying a beverage and snack is what made going to the airport fun. But 9/11 changed all that.

Instead of starting right in on the talk, Aunt Rose remained silent. She stood there looking straight at me, ever so tenderly. I was moved.

I picked up her bags, and we walked down the corridor and out the heavy revolving doors on the way to the car. Soon we were staggering out into the sunshine.

"How was your flight?" I asked.

"It feels like I've been sitting in an airplane for five days and five nights," said Aunt Rose. "We had a two-hour delay in San Diego before we even got started. Then a six-hour layover in Minneapolis to fix a mechanical problem delayed my flight to St. Louis."

"What were you doing in Minneapolis?" I asked.

"The direct flight from San Diego to St. Louis was full. To save money and catch a flight in the time range I wanted, transferring to a connecting flight in Minneapolis seemed to make sense when I was paying at the ticket counter," said Aunt Rose. "Bad decision. I could've traveled faster by riding the Pony Express."

"Once when I flew from St. Louis to New York–LaGuardia on an early-morning flight, the plane sat on the tarmac for an hour and a half, waiting for an attendant to find a new coffee maker inside the terminal and bring it to the stewardesses to replace the one that quit working," I said. "I guess the crew thought that taking off in an airplane full of passengers who were denied their morning coffee would be too much to bear."

"How is your mom?" asked Aunt Rose, as I loaded both suitcases into the back seat of my truck.

"She's slowed down a lot since last time you were here," I said. "I haven't draped my house in black yet, and your visit may raise her spirits. She always loves seeing her sister. My sisters and my girls are arriving later today. Do you want to head straight to Bethesda or stop at my house to drop off your luggage?"

"I can unpack later. Let's head straight to your mom's."

"Sounds good," I said.

A person could ask Aunt Rose anything. Her answers made sense. There was no need to have a complicated editorial translation. With her, life was real. It was made up of seconds, minutes, hours, and routines, cups of coffee, kindness, good intentions, bathroom breaks, and little things. There was never anything phony about Aunt Rose.

When we rolled up into the parking lot at Bethesda, trying to stay positive, Aunt Rose said, "I'll get to see how you guys decorated your mother's apartment. Last time I was here, I only saw an empty apartment version." We stepped from the car, and a day of full summer burst upon us with partly cloudy blue skies and intense heat that took on the added weight of moisture in the air, like a paper towel absorbing a spill on top of a hot stove.

As we entered Bethesda, I thought again about how amazing the place was. The caring was so evident, in big and small ways all across the campus. On days like this, it was a particular comfort. I knew Mom would be in good hands until the very end, when her comfort would be foremost, and kindness would surround her constantly on all sides. The approach to wellness by the people working at Bethesda makes the place one of the most remarkable senior living communities probably in the country. I was grateful we had found it.

When I entered Mom's room, her friends Helen and Loretta were already there. Mom lay on the bed. Her ankles had become swollen, probably due to water retention, poor circulation, and the new confinement of spending most of her time in bed. I was distressed that the ladies were talking so loudly, when Mom looked so weak and delicate. I tried to make shushing noises, but no one seemed to notice.

Mom glanced up at the voice that wanted her attention. She was lying there, her face squeezed and her lips tight, her arms pressed against the sheets to avoid any extra effort. She appeared to be lost in doctors' reports she could not follow and an end she could not pinpoint. She didn't know how much longer she could stand the state she was in. Bad news was starting to run through her veins like water flowing out a downspout.

"Stay strong, Audrey," said Helen.

"We will have to schedule a card game soon," said Loretta. She was a friend from Mom's old golfing days.

"We do what we have to do so we can do what we want to do," said Helen.

Nurses Gigi and Sylvia walked into the room and greeted Mom. She answered "hello," her one-word reply weak on both syllables.

"Gigi and Sylvia, these two ladies are friends of my mother," I said, introducing Helen and Loretta. All exchanged polite remarks, then Loretta asked Sylvia, "Do you get attached to your residents?"

"It's easy for someone to tell you not to get attached," Sylvia answered, "but it's hard not to in this work. Sometimes I get attached because the resident and their family have an effect on me. It was very easy to get attached to Audrey, because she is so intelligent and funny."

"People come into your life and you remember them for a reason, some purpose that may not be visible right away, but becomes evident later," said Gigi.

"Audrey allows herself to remain vulnerable and flawed and compassionate," said Sylvia.

A young woman from the kitchen staff rolled in a cart and placed a lunch prepared mostly of soft foods on a tray next to Mom's bed. I spoon-fed some of the lunch, now knowing which items my mother was still likely to try, things like pudding, yogurt, and ice cream. Water and orange juice were the only beverages she would drink.

The nurses continued to talk, and Aunt Rose and I murmured "oh" or "gee" at what we deemed the appropriate places. Mom's friends took on the glassy look of dutiful listeners. As the nurses talked, it was difficult for Helen and Loretta to break through the friendly chatter and understand the immediacy of the grave health condition of their friend.

After Mom signaled with hand gestures that she was finished eating, I pushed the food cart away from the bed. Mom's cheeks were the color of Crisco. Her hair was like grey thread knotted up in a ball, and her legs were thin as rolled-up newspapers. But none of that mattered. To my sisters and me, she was still our beautiful and trusted mother. I sat on the bed beside her, folding my arms and gripping my elbows, telling myself to stay calm and strong. A few moments later, Mom spoke.

"I want to see Patti. When is she coming to see me?"

"I talked to her on the phone two days ago," I said. "She probably would have been here by now, but she wanted to be sure the interstates were safe, so she was waiting until the thunderstorms passed through. The storms have moved out, so she's probably on the way here in her car. We should see her sometime tomorrow."

"Well," said Mom. "I just want everybody to get along. You all have to realize Patti is part of the younger generation. Let her do her thing. We need some younger energy helping out around here." After a few more minutes, she said, "You guys should all get some rest. Everybody can come back tomorrow." She squeezed my hand then instantly let it go, as if even that simple act was an exertion.

After saying goodbye, Mom's friends went home. Kathy and Aunt Rose slept at my house, and Patti, arriving in town during the wee hours, drove to her in-laws home in the suburbs to stay the night.

The next morning, as Kathy, Aunt Rose, and I neared the door to Mom's room in the hospice unit, we could hear Karen's voice inside. She was urging Mom to lie back in comfort on the new down pillows she had purchased from a home furnishings store.

"Mom, don't worry about anything. Just try to get some rest," said Karen, her words appearing calm and confident, trying not to show any fear of death or worry.

"Is my laundry finished?" asked Mom.

On the second Monday after Mom had moved into her apartment, someone from Bethesda's housecleaning crew had taped a sign next to the wardrobe chest that read: "Family Does Laundry." After many weeks of looking at the sign when bringing back heavy loads of laundered clothes, Karen grabbed a black magic marker, crossed out the word "family," wrote in her first name, and at the end of the phrase added: "on Thursdays."

"I allowed both loads of clothes to soak overnight," she was saying now. "That's why it took me almost three days to finish. The good news is that your clothes are super clean, soft, and have a fresh smell."

"Thank you," said Mom. "I need my clothes changed. Karen, do you know what to do?"

"I think so, Mom," said Karen. "I've been changing my own clothes for over five decades."

Karen closed the door and searched for the few items she needed from the laundry basket full of folded clothes, while everybody else waited in the adjoining room. Karen struggled to stop substituting words to help Mom speak, and Mom labored to quit offering motherly stories and making demands of Karen, mostly because both women had become accustomed to practicing this routine in recent junctures of their lives already. My mother and middle sister were working together in their personal space, like two competing championship skaters out on the ice alone, but without fanfare and without anyone watching. A few minutes later, as if the music ended and the ice-skating routine was over, Karen opened the door, while Mom rested on the bed wearing her clean new outfit.

Later in the morning, Karen had a meltdown. The strain of seeing Mom so ill was wearing on her, as it was on all of us, but Karen had a habit of cursing if she got upset enough. If she was in a bad mood, her anger would grow throughout the day. By evening, especially if she accidently did something like kick her big toe on a table leg, she would let loose with a string of cuss words that would impress a sailor. Added to Karen's worries about Mom was her anxiety over losing her job, which had happened several weeks earlier. She had been looking for work, with no luck.

A little while after dressing Mom, she broke down out in the hallway, outside Mom's door. "How the hell are my husband and I supposed to pay all our damn bills?" she burst out. "We're late on three utility bills."

Cursing and raising your voice at a place like Bethesda mixes about as well as oil with water. "My mother is dying, we can't pay the bills, and the world is turning to shit. What else is going to go wrong?" she cried, tears forcing their way out of her eyes.

Karen's flare-up was brief. At Aunt Rose's suggestion, she, Kathy, and I promised we would each give Karen fifty dollars to help her pay the overdue bills. When everyone was calm again, we soon were all back in Mom's room.

"Oh boy, what's going on?" Mom said when we stepped back in. "Why are so many people here at the same time?" She could see worried looks on our faces. She sat up in bed, her eyebrows arched, looking around for someone to explain.

"What's going on?" she asked again, reaching for a drink of water from a rose-colored cup.

"Mom, we're just trying to figure things out," I said.

"Maybe we should all start wearing rose-colored eye-glasses. I'm already drinking from a rose-colored cup," said Mom, in her down-to-earth way.

Joking eased the tension, and everybody laughed. The statement was typical of Mom. She always used humor to defuse a situation. Sensing the worry in the room, she had instantly shifted her mood from alarm to determination: she would put smiles on all her family's faces.

At that moment I remembered, as a choir boy, reading in the Roman Catholic Missal that the vestment color of rose, used at Mass during Advent, represented joy. Mom, in her ineffable way, was infusing joy and laughter into her hopeless situation, for the sake of the family she loved.

"Hi Grandma," said my daughters, Amanda and Allison, stepping through the bedroom door.

"Hi, sweethearts, I'm glad you're here," said Mom. "Allison, how long are you home from college?"

"My summer session classes are over and I get three weeks off," said Allison.

"Amanda, my dear, I love your shoes," said Aunt Rose.

"They're from Nordstrom," said Amanda.

"I thought they looked like shoes from Nordstrom," said Aunt Rose.

"Grandma, how are you feeling?" asked Amanda, leaning over to hug her grandmother.

"Oh, about the same," she said. "But seeing two of my granddaughters puts a smile on my face."

After everyone talked for a while, the dull look of suffering on Mom's face that had lifted as she talked to her granddaughters, settled again, grey and heavy like a concrete mold. Soon she nodded off and fell asleep.

"How are you holding up, Aunt Rose?" asked Amanda quietly, as Mom began snoring gently.

"Not too bad, under the circumstances. It's nice to see my great-nieces again. I wish we were together more often."

"I wish we were, too," said Amanda.

"I saw on Facebook that you went to Chicago to visit your high school friend Lisa. Did you drive or fly there?

How is Lisa doing?" I asked. "Did you guys do anything exciting in Chicago?"

"What's with all the inquiries? How about asking one question at a time?" asked Amanda, when my prying started to go too far.

"Dad, if I find that you are also stalking me, I'm going to have to delete you as my friend on Facebook," said Allison.

"Your dad is a talker, but you know he's not a stalker," said Aunt Rose.

Spending time with my daughters was enjoyable, even on a difficult day like this one. Talk that once might have triggered an argument when my daughters were younger, now incited laughter and further discussion. They had learned to express their opinions well, even if it meant a little teasing at my expense went along with their playfulness. Amanda and Allison were enduring the challenging situation of their grandma reaching her life's end, and their courage and good cheer brought a sense of pride to their father. I imagined myself living in an assisted care facility one day. Someday my daughters would care for me when I could no longer preserve my own illusions.

The way Mom woke from sleep set the tone for conversation with her. To start the conversation out right, Kathy or I would ask Mom a question designed to set her mind on positive things, usually: "Mom, what are the three things you are most grateful for in life?"

"My faith and my family," Mom would say almost immediately every time we asked her. Her faith and her family were always the first two things she mentioned. The third thing would vary, ranging from things like "my life with George" to "being with George in heaven" to "eating ice cream with friends." Sometimes that third thing just turned into a reminder to bury her in a certain favorite dress. There were no mentions of long walks in nature, or hobbies, or titles of helpful books she had read.

"Are you anxious?" I asked that afternoon when Mom woke up. I was responding to the tense look on her face.

"Yes, but . . ." said Mom.

"Not sleeping well?"

"Exactly. I have difficulty with anxiousness and sleep. I'm trying to keep it bunched up inside me, so I don't add worry to the rest of you."

"Do you know what day of the week it is today?"

"I'm not sure," said Mom.

"What month and year are we in today?" I asked.

"I'm not sure. Ask me an easier question," said Mom.

"Okay, what's your son's name?"

"Steve. I will never forget my son's name," said Mom, making her face remote and cross to make sure her remark wasn't ignored.

"I'm here with you until the end. I'm not about to leave you with two cigarettes and a glass of wine to fight your anxiety alone," I said.

It's wrong for anyone to blame another human being for accepting their finiteness, wanting a shortened process to their dying, instead of a lingering on for weeks or months in what they regard as useless suffering. At some point, all dying patients, after enough complications set in, give up hope. The term "passive suicide" is sometimes used, unfairly, when sick patients purposely break the rules to force a speedier end to living. While refusing medications, rejecting food, denying treatment, and refusing to drink water, a dying patient passively helps promote their own death.

When the pain starts to become unbearable, a dying person worries that their family will have to pay for the mounting expenses left behind. But the only focus should involve taking care of the physical (with strong pain medication), emotional, and spiritual needs of the dying person. Everything else is secondary.

"It's cold in here," said Patti, as she strolled into Mom's room through the hallway door. We had all been sitting there quietly, contemplating the future. Mom, in the next room, had dozed off again.

Everyone greeted Patti, and a hug fest ensured for several minutes. How good it was, to see all three of my sisters joining hearts in the common cause of taking care of Mom. It was the first time it had happened in a while, all four children reaching common ground together. After a few minutes, Mom woke up. She and Patti hugged, and both of their faces exhibited a special bond that needed no words to explain. The rest of us allowed Patti and Mom a few moments of private time together.

Emerging from Mom's bedside, Patti turned the thermostat up a few degrees and then turned on a lamp for added warmth. Outside the skies were partly cloudy; the green drapes on the long window were drawn wide open, allowing in light and a hope that the warming sun might neutralize the chill from the air-conditioning. But the tasks ahead for our family were more important than the temperature. Had it had been below zero or above a hundred, we were there to pull together to do what needed to get done.

The women in my family know how to take charge and get things done. They knew how to work alongside the professionals at Bethesda, because they had already learned to work as professionals in their own careers. If only the politicians stopped talking and took time to schedule a visit to Bethesda, I thought, they would learn a few things from all of these women about cutting through all the red tape. I was proud of my daughters and my sisters. In spite of the grief ahead that we would face together, our coming together that day felt like a great moment. Family provide such comfort in the bad times, and joy in the good times.

"I have to take a drive to the bank to cash a check," I said, after everyone had chatted a while. "Does anyone want to ride with me?"

"I'll ride with you, Dad," said Allison.

"I'll stay here to visit with Grandma and Aunt Rose," said Amanda.

"Okay. Allison and I will be back in a little while."

I drove the car to my bank, located on South Lindbergh Boulevard in St. Louis. With Allison sitting quietly in the front passenger seat beside me, I steered over toward a drive-up window. I inserted my signed check into a pink canister, pushed the button, and watched the canister shoot through a clear tube, like a potato chip being sucked up from a carpet by a vacuum cleaner.

"I think the blond woman working at the window is pretty and athletic looking," I said. "When I was younger, I always went for the girls who looked like tomboys."

"Dad, that's creepy. She looks like she is half your age," said Allison.

"I know she's too young for me. In any business relationship, participants have to act civil. There is nothing wrong with remaining friendly with people, no matter their age," I said.

"I have learned to read between the lines," said Allison.

"Maybe you're right. Maybe part of me is reverting back to thinking about the possibilities of the past. I'm just saying, if I was twenty years younger, the teller at the window is the kind of woman who would have caught my attention," I said. "She looks athletic, and I like her short blond hair."

"That's enough creepiness, Dad," said Allison.

A few seconds later, I heard the vacuum sound of the canister returning to the drop-down slot of the metal box outside my driver's side window.

"Thank you for banking with us," said the teller via her microphone. Let me know if we can do anything else to help you with your business needs."

Something weird came over me at that exact moment.

"There is one thing. If you would allow me, I would like to ask you a question," I said.

"Sure, go ahead," said the teller.

"My two daughters are younger than you, and they played softball and basketball in high school. What sports did you play?" I asked.

"I hate sports. I never played on any athletic teams in high school," said the teller.

"I'm sorry. Thank you for cashing my check," I said.

"Is there anything else I can do for you?" asked the teller in a crisp tone.

"That'll do it," I replied, as I always did when asked that question after making a deposit or cashing a check at the drive-up window.

Allison was unable to contain herself. She laughed all the way back to Bethesda, about a ten minute return trip from the bank.

"Steve, can you stay with Mom for two more hours, until you have to go to work?" asked Kathy, when we got back to the apartment.

"Sure. It's probably a good idea if we all start taking shifts, but we can talk about that later. You all should go home and get some rest," I said.

Mom raised her head, and it was a sad-eyed group when she addressed us in her cool but cracking voice.

"You can all go now. Steve, you should go home and get some rest too," said Mom, turning her head toward me.

"I feel pretty good. I'll stay for another hour or two. Then I have to leave to go to work," I said. "Aunt Rose, Kathy, Amanda, and Allison all have things they need to get done to prepare for tomorrow."

"Are you paying all the bills that are due?" asked Mom, looking straight at me.

"You have no reason to worry about the bills. I've paid all of them on time. Aunt Rose and the girls and I have everything taken care of and under control, because we have learned from our time together what needs attention, and usually without needing to ask each other anything. We have become a team," I said.

Aunt Rose and the girls left Bethesda. I was finally able to sit down to eat dinner at the table in the hospice visitor's space right outside Mom's room. I left the door to her room partially open and her television turned on, but with the volume turned down. That way, I could hear her if she needed something. Because of her condition, it would give me the willies to completely close a door with her on the other side. The television in the visitor's room was tuned to the same channel as the TV in the room where Mom was resting.

I made myself a salad from vegetables out of Karen's backyard garden. In the refrigerator of the visiting room, she had left cucumbers, tomatoes, carrots, and a small head of lettuce for me earlier in the day. She even included three packets of black pepper and a dry mix that only needed water to make the dressing for the salad. It takes work to grow a garden, but the reward of tasting fresh vegetables versus store-bought, canned, or frozen is tremendous. As I was enjoying every bite of my salad, a commercial aired on television showing starving children in Malaysia and other Third World countries. Since I wasn't the person who worked the garden to tender the vegetables I was eating for dinner, the guilt from the theme of the commercial about starving children halfway around the world seemed directed at people like me.

"Send . . . a . . . check . . .," said Mom, doing her best to speak loud enough for me to hear her in the other room. I heard her making noise, but I couldn't distinguish all the words she was trying to say. I stood up from the table and walked into her room to better hear.

"Send them a check for twenty dollars," said Mom, straining to grab my attention and express her wishes, staring at the television.

"Who, Mom, do you want me to send a check to?" I asked.

I imagined Mom telling me to finish my dinner first. The poor kids in China would never waste such a good meal. Because the door was partly open, she certainly saw me eating a salad. The television in her room was tuned to an old rerun of "Password" playing on the game channel. We hadn't changed the channel all day. We were hoping that the clothes the contestants wore on the old reruns might have brought Mom's mind back to happier times when Dad was still alive.

"Send a check to the food organization," said Mom, her raspy voice sounding as if she was irritated.

"Do you mean the one that just aired the commercial?"

"Yes," said Mom.

"I think it's called the World Hunger Organization to Save the Children," I said. "I saw the commercial, too, but I didn't catch their address or phone number. I'm sure I can find it on the Internet."

"I wish the Internet had never been invented," said Mom.

"Well, sometimes it's useful, Mom. An example is this here. The Internet is like having your own library, available right at your fingertips. You can find out almost anything you need to know," I said.

"I know, but the Internet is also responsible for igniting all the bad political movements around the world," said Mom.

"I'm not sure I believe the people in power who say the Internet is the most democratizing influence the world has ever known, because these same people have used the Internet to fuel the world's divisiveness," I said.

"Liberals are ruining our country," said Mom.

"Obama says net neutrality has been built into the fabric of the Internet since its creation," I said. "He says taking the Internet for granted is a mistake and the only way to keep it free and open is through government oversight."

"That sounds like an oxymoron," said Mom.

"I think you're right," I said.

"What's happening to our country?" asked Mom. "Too many things are changing all at once."

"All this rush for change has consequences," I said.

"When one political party rushes a big federal program through the system, without any output from the opposing party and without addressing important questions, the citizens pay the price."

"So much money is wasted," said Mom.

"We see higher costs and more of our freedoms taken away, while new protocol rarely makes anything more secure," I said.

"It all makes me sad," said Mom.

"Because of so many big changes, people will have less money to donate to charitable causes that work," I said.

"Promise me you will send the World Hunger Organization a check," said Mom.

"I promise. Tomorrow morning I will find their address on the computer and I will mail them a check," I said.

I didn't say it, but at the moment I was more worried about Mom not eating her meals than the children in Third World countries getting Mom's check for food. Mom had been eating almost nothing. I was hoping she would take at least a few bites of the food brought in to her room at mealtimes to alleviate her hunger pains, but the truth was that I was eating most of the food. When she did eat, she usually vomited.

"When I die, I want to be buried in my green dress and my string of pearls," said Mom, as she reached for her glass and devoured the water that remained in it with one desperate gulp.

She gave me one of her searching looks. I thought about making some excuse to push my chair back against the wall and leave for home, so I could avoid this conversation, but I decided to stay a while longer. We had not told Mom that the doctors said she was going to die.

"We will cross that bridge when the time comes," I said.

"No, now you know of my intentions. My green dress is still in the plastic from the last time it was brought here from the old house, and it's hanging in the closet behind you," said Mom. "My pearl necklace is in the wooden jewelry box inside the top drawer of my dresser."

I know it is said that just before the end, the minds of the elderly often revert back to memories of their childhood. Mom often spoke about her father, Harry, a good and intelligent man who worked hard and took care of his family before succumbing to cancer ten years prior to eligibility for retirement. Everything she told me about my grandfather pointed to his having been one of those courageous—if sometimes misguided, more often misinterpreted—types of men. He gave the pearl necklace to her on the day she married my dad. When she spoke about my grandfather, who died one year after I was born, I was unable to understand it all. But I knew, at least, the respect for him she had for the good things he did to support his family. She wanted to forget about the fact that he drank shots of whiskey every night during his later years, to ease his aches and go to sleep. For Mom's eternal rest, wearing her green dress and pearl necklace was not a stupid request; it was a serious sentimental demand.

Chapter 14

My family was experiencing a whole different kind of gridlock than the one in Washington. Aunt Rose, Kathy, and I were splitting shifts with Karen and Patti. Because my two youngest sisters had spent the midnight shift watching over Mom and helping the nurses attend to her needs, Aunt Rose and I took over in the morning and sent the girls home to recuperate.

The women in my family were all alpha females. My mother, Aunt Rose, my three sisters, and my two daughters all fit the definitions of forceful, assertive, competitive, and disruptive. But I am happy to say "disruptive" describes behavior they engaged in rarely, and only when they thought a greater good was to be served. On this occasion, everyone was trying hard to stay out of the way of the staff with their procedures, to be an adjunct in Mom's care, not a nuisance. Kathy, in particular, being a nurse herself, had to make an effort not to tell Mom's nurses how things ought to be done. All the ladies were behaving remarkably beautifully, especially considering the stress they all were under.

I leaned over and grabbed both of Mom's hands to help her sit up in her bed. She refused to speak right away. Then, reading my thoughts, she nodded her head, and pushed the bottoms of her feet against the floor. She slipped her arms around my neck and I pulled her up. We stood still together for a few moments, just the two of us, holding each other partially because of weakness, but more because of strength. I could feel her warmth despite the morning chill in the room. She drew a long breath trying to summon more energy, just as Aunt Rose scooted the portable toilet in place as close as she could next to the bed and behind Mom's legs.

"We have to turn and shuffle a few steps to your right," I said. "Let's concentrate on the task at hand."

"Shuffle, shuffle!" said Mom, as we were moving several short steps back and forth together to get where we needed to be.

"Shuffle, shuffle!" said Aunt Rose. "I'll get behind you Audrey, and help pull your pajama bottom down, so you can sit and go potty."

"Okay," said Mom.

"Good job. Now if you can just sit down slowly, I'll hold you tight until you are sitting comfortably on the seat. Then I will go wait in the hall," I said.

"I'll call for you to come back when we're ready for your help," said Aunt Rose.

Aunt Rose was right in telling my sisters and me to make sure we were getting enough rest. The days ahead would require extra demands on our minds and bodies.

Each day was about to become more demanding than the one preceding it, but nothing was beyond any one of us trying our best to shine a little light on any day that was full of darkness. It was easy for each of us to converse about simple things, like the similar pleasant taste between an almond and the fibrous white meat of a coconut. If anyone had asked us to, we probably could have found good things to say talking about piles of old rusty automobile parts, even after going without sleep for an entire night. Our goal was to make the atmosphere as pleasant for Mom as we could, and, with little discussion, we were tricking the coping mechanisms in our brains to work more efficiently. By talking brightly about life's little things, we were hoping to soften everything for our mother.

"Steve, you can come back in the room now," said Aunt Rose.

"Okay," I said, having just returned from grabbing a cup of coffee, one bottled water, and a cup of ice chips from the refrigerator in the gratuity lounge at the other end of the hall.

"Mom, do you think you have enough strength to sit in a chair for a few minutes?" I asked.

"I think so," said Mom.

Again we did our shuffling routine, and Mom was now sitting in the big green chair in the corner of the room. "Here is a cup of ice chips. Chewing on them should relieve the dryness in your lips. And here is a bottle of water for you, Aunt Rose," I said.

"Thank you, honey," said Aunt Rose.

A few hours later, after getting only a little sleep, Karen and Patti returned. Karen had washed more laundry for Mom and Patti had stopped to buy coffee and bagels for all of us.

"Thank you, Patti," said Kathy. "I've been craving a good cup of coffee all morning. My stomach is growling. I guess I'm hungry too."

"Thank you, honey," said Aunt Rose, reaching for a bagel.

"Everything we need is in the bag," said Patti. "There are four different kinds of bagels. I grabbed enough napkins, jelly packets, plastic knifes, and margarine at the coffeehouse. I bought two decafs and four regular coffees. I think I'm the only one who drinks decaf, but I bought one extra just in case. There are plenty of packets of sugar and containers of coffee creamer in the bag, too."

"This whole-wheat bagel with raisins looks delicious," I said.

"Add a little strawberry jelly, and it will taste ten times better than a fruitcake," said Karen.

"Anything is better than fruitcake," said Patti.

"Probably, but I could eat one of these bagels for breakfast every morning. It goes good with regular roasted coffee," I said.

Kathy was happy to finally have her cup of coffee. Aunt Rose suggested another bagel for me after noticing I finished eating the first one.

I could tell Karen was feeling quiet troubled, probably thinking about how she would no longer have the chance to talk with her mother after she was gone. The rest of us continued making small talk, speaking of pleasant things. I was trying to perform as the big brother, a leader—showing strength, and exercising enough wisdom to know when to listen, when to talk, and when to act.

"Kathy, how many days in a row are you going to wear that dress?" said Mom, back in bed, as Kathy walked past her. "I don't like it."

"Oh, gosh, Mom," said Kathy, embarrassed, trying to stare past Mom's comment, and hoping no one else had heard anything.

"Kathy is still wearing her beautiful matching nightgown and robe this morning," said Aunt Rose, "because she hasn't changed into her clothes yet this morning."

"Mom, every night Kathy changes into her set of nightwear so she is more comfortable staying overnight with you," I said.

"Moments like this will only give us more great memories," said Aunt Rose, amused.

Karen was filling a glass with water. The glass looked more like a fancy carafe than a regular drinking tumbler. Mom was feeling irritable now, and her words and tone sometimes showed it, but we all understood it was the pain that was talking. All her life, Mom's voice had been rich and controlled. She never raised it, even with her children, always hoping that her self-control would automatically mute us when we needed muting. She was happy when her family melded into one, as we were doing during these difficult days, because she believed when family members worked together, they opened huge pathways for outpourings of love, as if each person was freed by togetherness.

"A few more exchanges like that with Mom should allow us to maintain a fairly amiable environment in this room, said Karen, her comment drawing laughter from the rest of us. "Is it too early to pour wine into my fancy carafe?" and we laughed again.

We were slap-happy. Whatever anyone said seemed funny, and we laughed easily like children, maybe trying to mask our sadness and keep our sanity. We started talking about childhood memories and family vacations. Children never recall the buildings, the museums, or the décor of the hotels they stayed at on family holidays. They remember the silly and unexpected things that occurred when they were doing something that stretched their imagination. On one summer vacation, we drove all the way to Florida in a Ford station-wagon without air-conditioning because my father was determined to show his children the way people lived in Miami.

"I was nine then," said Kathy. "A stray dog appeared out of nowhere, and peed on my sandcastle. Steve scared Karen, because he said it was dangerous if you swallowed too much salt water when you swam in the ocean."

"Yeah, I remember. I told her if she swallowed too much salt water, her skin would wrinkle up and her bones would grow stiff, and her legs would hurt when she tried to walk."

"Why did you tell me that?" asked Karen. "Are you making that up, or did it really happen?"

"Do I dare theorize, when it comes to family vacations? Dad carried you out into the ocean to help you overcome any fear of the salt water. I know he was displeased with me for teasing and scaring you," I said.

"There's nothing better than walking along the ocean, the beach stretching as far as you can see," said Karen.

"The mist of the waves hitting you in the face, the warmth of the sand massaging your bare feet . . . the picture-perfect canvas of the surroundings within your touch—oh, my goodness, I love the ocean," said Aunt Rose.

Kathy brought up a story about our last summer vacation together as a family several years ago, when Dad was still alive.

"Remember that one day after breakfast when we went sailing on Kentucky Lake?" she asked.

"Are you talking about the time Mom sat on edge of the beach in the shallow water and watched the rest of us sail across the lake?"

"Yes. Dad stayed in his room at the lodge to watch golf on the newest thing in technology at the time, the flat screen," said Kathy.

"If I remember correctly, we were out on the water for about two hours," I said.

"When we started out, there was a slight wind, and we were gliding slowly across the water. Mom had our sailboat within her sights the whole time," said Kathy.

"I think Mom was happy wearing her bathing suit, sitting in the water, and just watching all the kids that were running around on the beach," I said.

"My step-son-in-law, Don, was doing the steering. The wind picked up and he said we should head back," recalled Kathy.

Don's sailboat was a thirty-foot sloop—old and slender, beautiful and reliable. The mast was patched with four rectangles of grey fabric against a white canvas that showed some yellowing from exposure to the sun and wind. Don sailed his magnificent boat as if he had lived on the water all of his life, which he had, since he had been barely able to walk. I figured that when he bought his first boat, he started small, because it takes experience to handle a full-sized sailboat. As a man's experience grows, so does his boundaries and the size of his boats. There are many steps between a Huck Finn existence and the knowledge needed to captain a sailboat across the ocean, or across a lake for that matter. If a boat is not maintained properly after each long outing, future sailing opportunities are lost, as the sailboat must stay in dry dock for long bouts of repair and restoration. But without those complications, we were blessed to have Don as our captain.

"Why the funny smile, Steve?" asked Aunt Rose.

"Was I smiling? I asked, looking up. "It was Mom I was thinking about. After we returned, we stepped off the sailboat at the dock, and walked over to join her. She was acting kind of funny. She said she was feeling feverish and dizzy."

"Do you think she was out in the sun too long?" asked Aunt Rose.

"Mom was wearing sunscreen. It wasn't until she took off her bathing suit and got into the shower that she figured out what had happened," said Kathy.

"May I finish the story?" I asked, hoping Kathy would oblige me.

"Go ahead," she said.

"Mom told us that when she bent down to turn on the water in the shower, she noticed half-a-dozen leeches clinging to her butt. Mom was embarrassed and flustered about the whole episode, but she managed to laugh along with all the mocking and teasing we floated her way," I said.

"Oh, my gosh," said Aunt Rose.

"I guess leeches like sucking blood from a leek with a nice butt," I told Mom, after we found out about her circumstance.

"Do you know what a 'leek' is, goofball?" Mom asked, giving me a chance to think about my use of that word.

"A 'leek' is a mature person," I told her.

"A 'leek' is a mature vegetable that resembles a thick green onion, you goofball," Mom said. I remember the glaring look she gave me as if she were still giving me that stare today.

"I think you like calling me a goofball," I told her. "Then

she asked me, would you like it better if I called you a 'leek'?"

"You kids should have known that when challenging your mother to a game of wits, she is always going to win," said Aunt Rose.

Mom had been dozing as we reminisced, but now I noticed she was awake. I walked over to her bed and was surprised to find her crying.

"For God's sake, Steve," said Mom. "Do you understand . . . exactly . . . what I want?"

"Yes, Mom," I said. "I know what you want."

"I'm asking you . . . to tell them to let me die."

Though I was hot, uncomfortable, and sleepy, I immediately came alert on hearing my mother's words. Here I was, the son she trusted to understand her as she understood herself. She wanted out of her suffering state. She wanted it to be over. I called Kathy over.

"Mom, it's crazy if you think that one of the nurses or Kathy or I can just grab a pillow, and when no one is looking, put it over your face and end everything for you," I said.

"That's one of the prevailing thoughts that keep occurring in my mind," said Mom.

"I knew that's what you were thinking," I said.

"Kathy, I just want to die," said Mom.

Nurse Susan walked in the room to help rescue us.

"Audrey, your doctor ordered this new air tank for you," she said. "It has a streamlined design and the plastic tubes are very light weight and fit around your ears. Hopefully, you will barely notice that the tubes supplying oxygen are hanging in front of your nostrils."

"Mom is extremely uncomfortable right now," said Kathy.

"The oxygen should help with that. I'm giving her another dose of pain medication. Her doctor has shortened the time between doses from every four hours to every three hours. If Audrey is sleeping, I won't wake her up to give her the medicine, but I'll keep checking on her."

Kathy and I decided to take a walk. We both needed to relieve the stress, and taking a walk usually helped calm our worries. As I followed Kathy out the front entrance and down the sidewalk. I sensed she was worried about something besides Mom.

"How is it going with the nurses you're training?" I asked her. "Are they keeping up with their work and studies without you there to supervise?"

"So far they are, but I don't know how much longer I can stay away before the higher-ups demand that I return. I guess I just have to keep faith that the other nurses will keep things going until I get back there," said Kathy.

"Nothing is easy right now," I said.

"I'm worried about Brad going off to college and leaving home for the first time, too," said Kathy.

"Dave can handle driving Brad down to Colorado Springs and can help him move his things."

"Sure, but I wanted to share the experience with my husband and son. But most of all, I'm worried about Mom, so everything else has to wait," said Kathy.

"I worry whether we're making the right decisions about everything. How long do you think Mom has left?"

"She may live a few more days, maybe a few more weeks," said Kathy. "She's eating so little. If I had to guess, I'd say one or two weeks."

"I guess I should coordinate arrangements with hospice and the funeral home," I said breaking into a sweat.

"Are you ready to do that, Steve? Funeral directors like it when they have extra time to prepare, but maybe we should just start with notifying friends and relatives, so they can plan."

"I'm okay," I said. "It needs to be done, and I'm ready to do it."

"It's probably a good idea."

"Mom made it a point to tell me she didn't want her dead body driven around in a gold limousine. She wants a black limousine," I said. "At least I'll be able to fall back on some of the experience I got when Dad died. Mom was a basket case at the funeral home then, but the men at the funeral home see every possible kind of response to grief there is, so they are very helpful. I think getting things started is the right thing to do. Maybe on a second visit, you, Karen, and Patti can come along and help me pick out flowers and styles and colors and ribbons and things," I said.

"I'd like that," said Kathy. She put on a burst of speed. "Come on. Your legs are only ten months older than mine, so keep up with me, or I'll send you to the cough room."

"What's the cough room?" I asked.

"You never heard of the cough room? Back in the sixteenth and seventeenth centuries, if a boy was sick with a cough, or acting out, or falling behind in his work, a schoolmaster or a doctor had the power to commit him to the cough room. That way, they hoped, the boy couldn't spread his disease or influence his bad behavior on other children."

I realized at that moment that Kathy is more like Mom than I had ever before taken the time to notice. She is a strong woman with determined cheerfulness and an unwavering cleverness, the two most needed virtues of any woman trying to keep a happy household. Talking to Kathy was easy for me, probably because she was my oldest sister, and closest in age to me.

"Visiting with Mom these last few weeks has been the longest stretch we've spent in the same room together since we were kids," said Kathy.

"I hope you mean that as a good thing," I said. She punched me in the arm.

"Lets walk a few more blocks to the top of the hill, then turn back," said Kathy.

"Did you know your maiden name, in German, means dweller on top of the hill?" I asked.

"Dad told us that story a hundred times," said Kathy.

When we got back to Bethesda, Aunt Rose was sitting there watching Mom sleep.

"How do you know a sick person is living their final hours?" I asked.

"When it gets real bad, their breathing sounds like the

rattle of a snake," said Aunt Rose. Aunt Rose knew, bless her heart, because both her husbands had died in her arms.

"Your Mom has all her children here now. That's all she wanted," said Aunt Rose.

That night when we left Bethesda, something was very different. We had spent hours trying to cheer up Mom. She ate very little, and when we spoke to her, her voice sounded hollow. Mostly when she wanted to speak, the words would not come out. Her blood sugar levels were through the roof, and her heart was working harder than ever. Her decline was a shock of the gradual kind, and our sorrow at knowing we were losing her went deep. I knew that I would never sit and talk with her again, never work together again to solve an unsolvable problem, never again discuss politics. It was clear to all of us Mom didn't have much time left.

Aunt Rose had called her cousin Peggy to tell her Mom was very sick. Peggy was an older cousin, and her sibling Sister Leonette, was the youngest cousin of Mom's and Aunt Rose's generation. After recently turning seventy, Sister Leonette had taken a position as a pastoral minister helping run a hospice program that offered in-home-services from an outreach office located a few miles southwest of the city of St. Louis. Just when our family needed it most, Peggy and Sister Leonette walked into the room to visit Mom. Because we all lived in different communities and all had our commitments, my sisters, Aunt Rose, and I saw these two ladies much less often than any one of us desired. Peggy nodded to all of us and walked directly to Mom's bed.

"It is nice to see you, Audrey," she said. "Sister Leonette is with me."

"Hi, Audrey," said Sister Leonette, leaning over to put her face close to Mom's.

"Nice . . . see . . . both," said Mom, struggling to sound her words.

"Hi, Rosie," said Peggy.

"Hi, Peg," said Aunt Rose.

"Rosie, how are you holding up?" asked Sister Leonette.

"Pretty good, Rita, considering everything."

Aunt Rose still called Sister Leonette by the name her parents gave her before she became a nun and the name she had called her by when they played together as little girls. She took the religious name, Leonette, in honor of her father Leo, a sweet man she admired immensely. By taking the female version of his name, she wanted to dedicate her life's work praising God in memory of her father's goodness.

"Let's offer a prayer to God," said Sister Leonette, and we all gathered around Mom's bed. "When we praise God for all of his works, we are giving Him our blessings. It's a heartfelt response to His gifts. He grants us a dialogue because He is the source of everything. When we give homage to the Creator of all, we are professing our adoration of Him. We express our love and devotion because God is our joy and our hope," said Sister Leonette, guiding us in prayer.

After the praying was finished, we settled in and sat at the round dining table in the adjacent sitting room to talk. From the kitchen, Kim sent us a cart full of snacks and succulent pastries. While the rest of us ate, Kathy stood in the hall discussing Mom's pain medications with the nurses. I liked watching her interact with them, seeing in her mannerisms, things that reminded me of Mom and things that reminded me of me. I loved my sisters both for the ways we were the same and the ways we were different. I loved them for their kindness, their creativity, their intelligence, and the love and devotion they bore our mom. Love is untrained, but the adoration a man has for the caring women in his life grows to endless heights and is often hard to explain in good times, but probably even more so in bad times.

"Your mother has reaffirmed her faith," said Sister Leonette.

"She let go of all her worldly possessions several months ago," I said.

"Everything superficial has been bleached clean, and only the essential things matter to her now," said Sister Leonette. "All that matters is that Audrey has control of her situation and is allowed to focus on the sustenance of her soul and die in peace."

"I'm proud of all four of you guys for staying in the trenches every day, fighting for your Mom," Aunt Rose said. "Not one of you will have to feel any guilt for failing to react to her needs in her most difficult hours."

Inside the walls of Bethesda, there were faces the family knew and faces only Mom knew from living there. Some walked between the same rows of chairs she did on Tuesday nights as she went to play Bingo in hopes of winning a bag of pretzels or some small monetary amount. There was the heavy lady down the hall who found it nearly impossible to control her weight because of all the medications she had to take every day. She spent hours in the morning doing her makeup, hoping other residents would like her. There was the elderly man who lived in another wing of the building. He had an ugly scar on his face, but he was respected, partly because he received his wounds fighting for his country. There was the elderly lady that lived three doors down from the elevator that I saw crying once because she was sad from just finding out that her best friend ever since childhood had died. Soon my days at Bethesda would be over, and the residents and staff would flow out of my life. Bethesda had become a part of me and I was going to miss it.

Chapter 15

I t was the beginning of the second week of August, a Sunday night, and the air outside was hot and humid. But an intense environment always became cooler when Sister Leonette walked into a room, and this time she brought her associate, Sister Donna, to visit with us. Whenever Sister Leonette made a social call, her visit always included a reading from the New Testament and a prayer that required a response from whoever was present.

As I watched my mother's eyelids flutter and her mouth hang open miserably to let air trickle in and out, I was certain she was more alone in the world than others were willing to admit. But in another way of looking at the situation, the only thing she needed was the people close to her offering her love and comfort. The two nuns arrived at the perfect time.

"Lord, guard us and guide us through any difficult hours of darkness," prayed Sister Leonette in a low, soft tone, as Mom half-dozed in the bed. "Thank you, Audrey, for doing your best to live a faith-filled life, by remaining a great example to your children and loved ones. Now it is our turn. Please, Lord, help us find the patience that Audrey would want from all of us. In waiting for anything you really want, the taste is sweeter when waiting requires a high level of patience."

"Lord, hear our prayers," said Aunt Rose, Kathy, and me, as we responded to Sister's humble request.

After briefly stepping out of the room to discuss Mom's pain medications with the nurses again, Kathy and I could hear Sister Leonette and Sister Donna warming up their voices. We walked back into the room and saw Mom awake and propped up, watching the nuns.

Sister Leonette placed a CD into a portable recorder and began strumming guitars. As their singing began, patients and staff shuffled into the room, staying to listen. I brought in a chair from the hall so Aunt Rose could sit close to her sister and enjoy the proceedings from a front-row seat.

"Go on and sing along," said Aunt Rose to Mom, encouraging her.

Mom stared at the two singing nuns, unblinking and watching their every movement, listening with her eyes as well as her ears. With her mouth, she was trying her best to lip-sync a few of the main words from repeated choruses. I don't know if we were witnessing musical genius, but when the song "Amazing Grace" started playing, and the nuns ramped up their voices to join in the song, something inside me tugged at my soul, as I felt suspended. It was like a little taste of heaven. "If you like what you see, take me with you, God," I prayed. "Don't send me back, but if I must go back, teach me to walk in Your ways. I will work hard for you." Then suddenly reality pulled me back to the here and now of my life on Earth.

When the music finished, Sister Leonette turned to the visitors in the room. "Thank you all for joining us, and keep praying for my cousin, Audrey," she said.

"Thank you, Sisters, for singing and playing your guitars so beautifully," said Aunt Rose, gentling bowing toward the nuns.

Thank God for volunteers like Sisters Leonette and Donna. They turn their faces away from the ugliness of death and create something of beauty and grace in a space where there is a need for it. They play at skilled nursing and assisted living facilities, and at hospitals and hospices. Their music helps people struggling with Alzheimer's, dementia, strokes, and dying to reconnect with the world through music-triggered memories. Through their energy, enthusiasm, and a lot of hard work, they are attempting to make music a standard of care throughout the health care industry in St. Louis. God bless them for their efforts.

It was about an hour before midnight when the door closed on Aunt Rose and me. The nuns gone home, Kathy left to go get some sleep at my house, and the residents went back to their rooms. It was clear that this night would lead to more nights at Mom's bedside. We just didn't know how many. Aunt Rose and I sat and talked patiently, drawn to an electronic picture frame on the wall. The picture inside the frame was of a tree with leaves that changed colors and dropped off its branches each day, symbolic of departure from earth to a greater place of eternal rest.

"What are you thinking about?" I asked, looking directly at my aunt.

"Tonight was a wonderful evening. Your mom wore that look on her face all evening, the one that said she loved every moment of her special party."

"I'm thinking about how peaceful the room is right now."

"We had a great night praying and singing with the sisters. I will remember it for the rest of my life."

The room was now quiet. I watched Mom stretch and quietly groan in bed, before rolling over onto her other side. Aunt Rose pushed back the handle on the recliner she was sitting in, elevated her legs, fell back against the headrest, and closed her eyes.

The next afternoon, Mom seemed even sicker than before. There was no more turning back the clock or fending off illness. There were no longings for anything of Earth, only disgust for the slow passage of time. There were no more reasons for hope of recovery. We were looking out at the darkest hours ahead, the kind filled with grief and sadness. Each member of our family was trying to find their own best way to grieve. The kitchen staff kept bringing meals to the room on trays, mainly to stay compliant with healthcare laws, but Mom just looked at the plates as if she didn't know for sure what they were there for anymore. A small bowl of chocolate pudding and a glass of water stood on a tray next to her bed, but Mom no longer thought about food.

Kathy and I did our best to help Mom understand that her grandson, Brad, was on his way to Bethesda for a visit. Brad's last day of summer lacrosse coincided with his father's last day of meeting with contractors to finalize a concrete project for a new driveway and sidewalk at their house in Denver.

"So Mom, Dave and Brad left yesterday morning from Denver, and they are due any minute now. They brought the dogs, Sadie and McKenna," Kathy told her.

We kept listening for the first sound of their SUV roaring up the hill to the main entrance. It was nearly one in the afternoon when we saw them pulling into a parking space outside the building.

Brad saw me at the window. Gripping a leash in each hand, he commanded, "Down," as one of the golden retrievers lunged unexpectedly. The two dogs looked alike, and it was difficult for me to tell them apart, especially from far away. Brad walked the dogs across the grass, over to our ground-floor window. He was hoping his grandmother could see them one more time. My sisters were calling out silly remarks now, through the window.

"Hi Brad, nice athletic shoes," said Kathy. "Have you missed your mother?"

"Yes, Mom," said Brad.

"Hi, handsome," said Karen.

"Hi, Aunt Karen," said Brad.

"How do you know whether I was talking to you or one of those good-looking dogs?" asked Karen.

Watching Dave and Brad, father and son, try to make something better of a situation that they were barely able to accept, was heartwarming for the rest of the family watching.

After putting his dogs back in their pens in the back of the SUV, Brad came into the building and hurried into the outstretched arms of his grandmother. Dave and Brad knew they had arrived toward the end of the game, and despite the sadness of everything, nothing they could do was going to change the outcome for Mom.

That evening, after dozing for a while, Mom woke, and with one of her hands pinned beneath her, tried to straighten up and reach for a cup of water on the table next to her bed. I hurried over.

"Drink this, Mom," I said. "Can you hold the cup?" I tried to place it in her hands, but for the first time, she lacked the strength to hold it. I held it to her mouth. For the first time, she lacked the ability to swallow, choking on the water. I quickly pulled the cup away and set it back on the table.

"Mom, do you know what day it is?" I asked.

"No," she said, one syllable sounding like an hour's worth of effort.

I listened, giving her more time to think. It appeared she wanted to say more.

"Is it someone's birthday?" she asked, struggling

mightily to get all four words out, and putting a smile on my face.

"No, Mom, it's just another Monday night," I said, realizing as soon as the words left my lips, that any of the hours or days we had left would never be regarded as regular or average, because we were at the end.

"Mom, do you know that you are dying?" I asked.

"Who's dying? Steve is dying," said Mom, a confused look on her face.

"Audrey, my dear sister, you are still making us laugh," said Aunt Rose.

"Mom, I talked to Sister Leonette on the phone yesterday. I also talked to Laurel who runs the hospice program hear at Bethesda," I said.

"I know," said Mom, pausing and trying to muster enough energy to speak, "that I'm dying."

"I'm on board, if you are on board with the hospice program," I said.

"The good thing is we have professionals who will continue to monitor your pain," said Kathy. "You will receive stronger doses of pain medication if you experience any elevated amounts of discomfort." I could tell from Kathy's face that she was choking back emotion, trying to show strength.

"Just know you are surrounded by all the people who love you," said Aunt Rose.

"I'm ready," said Mom, nodding, then closing her eyes.

After that conversation, there was no need to mince words around Mom or to worry if we might frighten her by talk of dying. Our wish was the same as hers now, a plea for eternal peace. She deserved all the grace, warmth, and dignity we could muster.

It was early in the morning the next day when a certified nursing assistant named Kelly showed up in our room. Kathy, Karen, and Patti were there to relieve Aunt Rose and me. We all watched as Kelly stripped the blankets and sheets down with one sweep of her hand on one side of the bed, bunched the bedding materials into a roll, and then pushed the bundle up close against Mom's body while she was still lying in the middle of the mattress. Kelly then gently rolled Mom over the rolled up bundle and onto her side. Then Kelly walked over to the other side of the bed, rolled up the parts of linens still connected to the mattress, and stripped away the bedding completely. Within moments she showed us an easy way to change the bed sheets and blankets while barely moving the person in bed. It was a safe way for one person to change the bedding alone.

"You just trained my sisters and me in a new procedure that makes changing sheets, adjusting the bed, and fluffing the pillows much easier," I said.

"I was told Kathy is a nurse in Denver," said Kelly. "I'm sure she knows this procedure."

"Yes, but I think you do it much faster than I do," said Kathy.

"I have become adept at it because I change so many linens everyday. If your Mom had still been asleep, I could have changed the bedding without waking her," said Kelly.

The air was now heavy and sullen outside, the way it usually is during the sweltering month of August in St. Louis, but inside, the atmosphere was light and calming, thanks to the gentle mood Kelly set for our family. Now with all new sheets and linens on her bed, Mom was resting comfortably. She was resigned to what was coming, and by putting all her trust in God, she was showing her family that she courageously accepted her fate.

But impending death was a curiosity that was forcing me to think about weird things, because of all the unknown intangibles about the afterlife. Thinking about death is like chewing on a big piece of gristle from a porterhouse steak. You wish the unpleasantness of the taste never happened, and your next reaction is to spit it out. But bizarre thoughts of death, when a loved one is dying, are hard to get rid of. I found myself wondering how many months it takes for a dead body to transform into a skeleton, and how many years before a skeleton turned to dust. What was wrong with me? My mother was still alive, and I hated that these thoughts had entered my mind. Maybe my brain was overloaded or maybe I was just tired.

"What are you thinking about?" I asked Aunt Rose, as we drove back to the house to get some sleep.

"I'm thinking what a rich life my sister had and what good lives she and I shared as children. Plenty of classmates came from wealthier homes than ours, but they never had the closeness and the richness that we shared," said Aunt Rose.

"As if you were twins," I said.

"My big sister was full of passion and compassion, the two things every person needs to live a fulfilling life."

"I would need a very thick notebook to list all the things she taught me," I said.

That evening, when we returned to Bethesda, Mom had a visit from Nurse Sylvia. We had not seen her since Mom had been transferred out of Sylvia's assisted living wing to the hospice unit.

"I'm on break, so I came by to visit with one of my favorite residents," said Sylvia.

"You are so sweet," said Aunt Rose.

Sylvia walked right over to Mom, lay down next to her on the bed, and placed her arm around her.

"Audrey, I hear you are staying on this side of the building now," said Sylvia.

"Yeah," said Mom, mumbling her answer as if half asleep.

"You make sure the nurses over here take good care of you. If you have any complaints, tell Steve or one of your daughters to come get me. I will make sure to tell the other nurses to do whatever it takes to help keep you comfortable," said Sylvia.

Mom opened her eyes, looked at Sylvia, and nodded. She was making an effort, and I was so proud of her.

Perhaps no aspect of medical care is more precious than hospice care. Hospice is the personal decision to optimize quality of care, minimize pain, and provide comfort for a loved one when he or she is faced with a prognosis that offers no chance for recovery. It takes an honest realization from the family that all involved will work together to minimize the symptoms of disease rather than continue searching for a cure. Some families make the mistake of not considering hospice care, because they think they are "giving up." The truth is that hospice is about family members living each day to its fullest, when a loved one is faced with a life-ending illness. Hospice is about neither shortening nor prolonging a life. It's about making the transition a peaceful one.

The next morning, Sister Leonette brought a case of small glass bottles, one filled with linseed oil and others with the musk of various herbs. Sister used the substances to anoint Mom's forehead and provide clean scents to the air in the room. It was great seeing our mother resting comfortably, soothed by Sister's visit. A soft cotton blanket lay over her, and Kathy had put a new pair of thick foot-warmers on Mom's feet.

One by one, the grandchildren walked into the room and went through the misery of saying goodbye to their grandmother. First Amanda shared her love and private thoughts with her grandma. Then Allison took her turn. Allison brought her boyfriend, Justin, along to introduce to her grandma for the first time, and he was met with a wink of approval. Maybe Justin's big blue eyes reminded Mom of the early days when she was being courted by my father, or maybe she just believed in her granddaughter's choices. Brad went next to hug, kiss, and cry alone with the one person in the world, other than his parents, who had shown him so much love. Then Patti and Hoff's daughter Sydney, then their son Connor, here for the first time at Bethesda, already grieving for the inevitable loss of the closeness they had with their grandma. They must have noticed the troubled looks of the older adults. I noticed the awkward silences about them, their difficult stares, and their tongue-tied, uncomfortable reactions. Walking away from the bedside, each of the grandchildren burst into tears.

Just after midnight, hospice nurse Susan crushed a pill into a glass of water in a tiny white paper cup.

"Here, Audrey, you need to take this pill. It will make you more comfortable," she said, holding the cup to Mom's lips.

Mom nodded her head in agreement, but swallowing was very difficult for her. After several tiny sips, she managed to drink the prepared mixture. It was the first dose of morphine given to my mother. Taking medication was different now from earlier days when she might delay or consider disobeying the instructions of the nurses when they had their backs turned. As long as the mountains of hurt rising through her legs and arms and neck were eased by pills, she would gratefully take them. Mom no longer needed doctor's explanations about her conditions. Her body was giving her the only important information she needed, and all she was hoping for were that things would occur easier, faster, and surer.

"The first dose of morphine should help Audrey sleep through most of the night," said Nurse Susan.

"Good," said Aunt Rose. "Thank you."

"I'll come back in an hour to check on her."

"Thank you, Nurse Susan," I said.

"A month ago, Mom was still walking down the hall using her cane, and talking to other people, though she needed help tying her shoelaces," I said to Aunt Rose, after the nurse left the room.

The next day, Helen came to Bethesda to visit Mom. When she appeared in the doorway, my eyes were trying to signal a warning to her. Part of me wished I could give her more details, comfort her, and tell her much more about so many things. But another part of me, the sensible part that my father worked hard for so many years to instill, told me not to say too much. Helen was about to lose her best friend, and saying the wrong thing would make things worse for her.

"How are you, Audrey?" said Helen to Mom, who was barely awake.

"She is sleeping most of the day, now," said Aunt Rose.

"Audrey, you have to feel better soon. We have our card game with the girls next week," said Helen.

"No, we are further along now," muttered Aunt Rose under her breath, making a snuffling sound, holding back tears.

Helen looked at me, a question in her eyes. I could see she was hurting. She was unsure what to say or ask or if there was something she might do that would help.

"The nurses started Mom on morphine last night. At this point we're just trying to keep her comfortable. Hopefully, she will sleep most of the day," I said.

"This is hard for me," said Helen.

"I know, honey," said Aunt Rose.

"Helen and Mom always had such fun when they hung out together," I said. "Helen brought books to Mom for her to read, and she crocheted a hat for her last fall that Mom wore all winter."

Helen was clearly struggling to accept what she was seeing. There were many things that Helen and I would have to get used to and do without in coming weeks and months.

"One day each of us will simply go to sleep and not wake up," said Aunt Rose.

"Did you know, Rose, that Audrey and I lost our husbands in the same year?" asked Helen, her voice shaking.

"Yes, I heard that. I'm very sorry," said Aunt Rose. "I'm glad that you and my sister could lean on each other for support."

"I hope God is forgiving, especially for my husband," said Helen.

"I lost two husbands, both due to heart disease. Both of my husbands died in my arms," said Aunt Rose.

"I'm sorry, Rose. I would never say anything to purposely bring on more hurt. I'm always saying the wrong thing. When I was with your sister, she would always mop up after me. She always made things right," said Helen.

"Audrey could outwit the devil himself," said Aunt Rose.

I saw Helen's pain. Although she had difficulty understanding it all, I nodded to her respectfully, and then to

Aunt Rose, who smiled back at me.

"Well, I'm going to leave now," said Helen.

"Helen, take care," said Aunt Rose. "Thank you for visiting."

"Helen, let me walk you to your car," I said.

Helen and I walked carefully so as not to slip on the freshly mopped hallway. We veered towards a side door, the exit closest to where Helen had parked her car. Pushing open the bar, but not noticing the small sign at the top of the door, I set off the emergency alarm. My flawed judgment could have easily set off a panic in me, but somehow the unexpected event added a little momentary color to the day. Suspense is inherent in such a situation. Out of the side of her mouth, as she brushed past me and took a step outside the forbidden door, Helen let go a two-word expletive. Luckily, a maintenance worker standing nearby saw our mishap, maybe even anticipated it. He pulled out a set of keys from his pocket, quickly found the one he needed, and disengaged the alarm within half a minute.

"Sorry about that," I said.

"Sir, this is an emergency exit," said the maintenance man.

The unintentional mishap saved Helen a long walk around the building to get to her car. As the worker pulled the door closed behind me, I walked back down the hall, smiling. The embarrassed smirk stayed on my face until I was back in Mom's room.

I understood now that it was Mom's party, even though she was no longer curious about the world outside of Bethesda, and no longer able to muster the energy to ask many more questions. It didn't matter, in these days, if I made a mistake like setting off an emergency alarm. The only important job left for me now was to go with the flow. It was as if Aunt Rose, my sisters, and I were all children again and none of us had anything to apologize for anymore.

The first dose of morphine had worked with profound effects. When she finally fully awoke, she insisted that I help her sit up on the edge of the bed. She wanted to walk.

"Am I getting better?" asked Mom.

"No, strong medication is giving you a false sense of healing. Morphine does that to patients," I said.

"The nurses are giving it to you to alleviate your pain," said Aunt Rose.

"Try to relax, Mom," I said.

"Just imagine that you are walking along a wooden floor, hand and hand with George, all alone on the dance floor and your hair blowing in front of a fan. And George notices your beautiful hair," said Aunt Rose.

"I want to get up and try to walk," said Mom.

"All we need is for you to fall and break your hip," I said. "That would be a disaster."

Because she insisted that I allow her a chance to prove that she could walk, I lifted her frail body, positioned her arms around my neck, and sat her in position on the edge of the bed. She looked at me and then away. I held her tight, lifted her straight up, and allowed her to place both feet squarely on the floor. As we stood in place, most of her weight was balanced between my arms, like a wet noodle on two prongs of a fork. She bowed her head to hide her face in disappointment. Then she put her hands on my shoulders and said, "I need to lie back down," as if a million nerve endings confirmed what I told her. Mom was unable to move her feet. The small tasks of sitting up and trying to walk were enough to tire her. In less than two minutes, she was asleep again.

Mom was tired, and we could feel her strength draining completely away. She had stopped fighting. She just wanted to close her eyes, thinking that if she went to sleep this time, she would travel with God to go see her husband George and stay with him forever. She had overcome incredible depths and had reached incredible heights. But now even whispered words made her head hurt. Even with the thin tubing from an oxygen machine wrapped around her ears and plugged into her nose, she struggled to breathe. Every time the nurses checked vitals, the monitoring showed that her heart was racing harder. God was waiting to take her soul.

"I'm thinking about how peaceful it is in the room right now," said Aunt Rose, after Mom had fallen asleep. "In a mysterious way, the last weeks have been wonderful. If your mother could still talk, she would tell each of you how proud she was of her family."

"We are all walking around like zombies, but you are right. The whole experience this year at Bethesda has turned into one of the most special times of my life," I said.

"I'll remember the nuns singing, and my sister trying

to lip-sync the words to the songs, for the rest of my life," said Aunt Rose.

"Because of your skills and the highly trained professionals around here, half the time no one even needed to speak a word to ask for something," I said. "Aunt Rose, I sincerely appreciate everything you have done for our family."

"Audrey is my sister," said Aunt Rose. "I love her."

During their entire sisterhood, Mom and Aunt Rose loved life. Both women worked hard to overcome challenges, facing problems head-on. There was always time left to laugh and enjoy each other's company. When Aunt Rose moved to California, she made it a routine to telephone her sister every weekend.

Mable walked into the room to check on our family.

"Stable Mable restocking the snacks on the table, while we're listening to the newscaster on cable telling us a fable," I said, then immediately second-guessed myself. I hoped that I sounded clever and funny, not disrespectful or mean. I was surprised at some of the stuff that was coming out of my mouth uncensored. The stress was showing on me.

"Thank you, Mable, for taking care of us and for making sure we had enough to eat and drink the last few days," said Aunt Rose, softening my glibness.

"Sure. It's been my pleasure," said Mable. "Kim's kitchen staff is short-handed because two employees took their vacation time. I'm filling in and working extra hours to help out, so you're seeing a lot of me."

For the rest of the evening Mom slept. She looked as neat and cozy as a baby wearing a fresh gown tucked inside crib made up with clean cotton sheets. I know how she looked and how she felt were opposites and was glad she was sleeping through what had to be the worst part of her ordeal so far.

Nurse Susan walked into the room to observe her patient and check vital signs.

"Audrey is resting comfortably now," she said. "Every four hours, we will administer another dose of morphine by this I.V. to keep her comfortable."

"If she is sleeping, do you have to wake her to administer the medication? Can you wait until she opens her eyes?" I asked.

"We might not see her open her eyes again," said Aunt Rose.

"We are monitoring how Audrey moves her extremities in bed," said Nurse Susan. "We're doing our best to manage her pain. When she gets restless, we know the effects of the drug are wearing off."

"I guess that's the main thing, no more pain," I said.

"Tomorrow the nurses will make plans for stronger doses of medication. Because she quit ingesting food five days ago and no longer can swallow water, she would suffer tremendous discomfort without strong medication," said Nurse Susan.

One or more of us ventured in and out of the room every fifteen minutes to check on Mom. Only the bathroom separated her resting area from the sitting room where we waited and talked. By keeping the doors open on each side of the bathroom, we could see through to her bed and hear any sounds or see any movements that might indicate she was needing or asking for anything.

Kathy and Patti walked in, looking tired.

"I just talked to Nurse Susan in the hall," said Kathy. "I asked her if we could do something about Mom's dry mouth and chapped lips."

"What did she say?" I asked.

"She gave me these sponge sticks to try. They might give some relief. She said when a person has trouble swallowing, they sometimes try using them. They are just popsicle sticks with a small sponge on one end. You dip it in cold water, then hold it to Mom's lips and let her decide if she wants to suck on it. If she responds favorably, we'll keep using them," said Kathy.

"There is something else we need to start doing," said Aunt Rose. We must let people know your mother is in the final stage of hospice. We need to tell them to keep an eye out for the obituary in the newspaper. I'll go through her personal phone book and make a list of friends and relatives we need to notify."

"If you and each of my sisters each tackle a few names, you guys should be able to contact all the people we need to call," I said.

"We must contact her friends, and members of both sides of the family," said Aunt Rose. "I'm not sure where they all live, but I think most of their names are listed in her little blue phone book."

"Some of her friends never visited Mom at Bethesda, but that is probably because they have health problems of their own," I said. "Some of her friends are as old as she is or older. One woman in her bridge group is ninety-five. She needed a little help analyzing her cards when they played on Tuesdays."

"When I talk to Helen and Loretta, I'll check with them to see if we missed anyone from their group that we should call," said Aunt Rose.

"That's a good idea. Helen and Loretta know all the people from the old golfing group and the people who still play cards regularly," I said. "I'll leave the phone calls up to you guys tonight, because I need to go home and change into other clothes and go to work. I'll see you all tomorrow."

It was a good time for me to leave anyway. The nurses would soon give Mom a sponge bath in bed, turning her from one side to the other. Kathy would stay busy helping and washing Mom's hair with a waterless shampoo that made even the room smell grand. Patti would make sure to change the pillow cases. Karen would lay out fresh laundered nightwear and drive to a florist to pick up fresh flowers for the room. Nurse Susan, Aunt Rose, and my sisters had everything down to a science.

Nine years earlier I did more of the personal hygiene type of things for my dad, when he was sick. I remember shaving his face very carefully so as not to cut him with the razor. His cancer was doing enough damage to the other parts of his body. Though Dad died, he is always with me. He and Mom are the place I came from, and my first trusted friends. Nothing on Earth can take away that bond—not time, not space, and not death. Parents are the memory of certain foods that they cooked in the kitchen. They are the magic that healed your pain growing up when you were hurt. And when they are gone, they still influence your thinking. Those memories of our parents always remain in our hearts after they leave this world.

Before heading out to work, as the sun was low and hiding, I drove to the convenient mart in my neighborhood for a cup of coffee. The wind was blowing, and the clouds were darkening. It was turning out to be an awful evening in every way. Before leaving my house that morning, I had loaded a commercial weed-eater and a backpack blower into the bed of my truck and had covered both pieces of equipment with a plastic, tied-down sheet, in case the weather forecasters were right in their prediction of an oncoming storm. I spent about five minutes inside the convenient mart making my cup of coffee and standing in line to pay for it. When I stepped outside again, the rain was coming down. In the few seconds it took to walk from the store to my truck, all the clothes on my body got soaked. I was about to open the door of my truck on the driver's side when I glanced back to see if the plastic sheet was keeping my equipment dry. The weed-eater and backpack blower, for which I had paid $600, were gone. In the short time I had been inside the store to buy a cup of coffee, a thief had stolen my equipment.

The loss, on top of the sorrows of the day, filled me with

despair. If I was younger or wimpier, I might have started to cry. I used that weed-eater to eliminate the grasses and weeds that grow in the cracks along curbs and sidewalks near entrances to buildings. I used the backpack blower to blast away grass clipping, leaves, and tree debris to improve the appearance of landscapes at properties. It felt like a violation that this had happened. For several miserable moments, I felt like everything in the world was out to get me. I forced myself to buck up.

I knew that the local Home-Depot stayed open late, so I headed there to purchase new equipment. Within about twenty-five minutes, I was at the cashier's desk paying for a new weed-eater and backpack blower, similar models to the ones that had been stolen. I felt like weeping again when I handed the cashier my credit card. Under my breath, I whispered, "I hope that someday someone catches that asshole."

"What did you say?" asked the cashier.

"Oh, nothing. I'm talking to myself," I said.

"People do that when they get older," said the cashier.

"You are right about that," I said.

I didn't want to tell her my story about the thief who breached my faith about how in hard times we must rely on the goodness of strangers. Telling the cashier about my misery and disappointment in my fellow man, would only add discomfort to her day.

"Sir, here is a $25 gift card," she said. "We are giving out the gift cards, this week only, to any customers who spend $500 or more."

"So we *can* still rely on the goodness of strangers," I muttered. "Actually, I knew that already. There are some wonderful people working at Bethesda on Telegraph Road."

"What? You lost me there," said the cashier.

"Just know that you brightened my day. Thank you for the gift card," I said.

The cashier handed me my receipt, and I wheeled the shopping cart with my two newly purchased items out of the store. Before I stepped into my truck and drove away, I whispered under my breath one more time, "I hope that someday someone catches that asshole."

Back at Bethesda the next day, I decided not to tell my family what had happened to my equipment. All of us had enough on our minds, enough other things to prioritize and worry about.

"Hi guys," said Nurse Susan to Aunt Rose and I as we passed her in the hall on the way to Mom's room. "Audrey slept most of the night, but she experienced some restlessness just before she was due for another dose of her medication. Today at noon, we're hoping to start even stronger doses of morphine. I'm waiting for approval from her doctor."

Before we could say anything, Nurse Susan's cell phone started beeping.

"Hi doctor. I guess you received my message. Steve and Audrey's sister Rose are here standing right next to me," said Susan.

"Tell Dr. Calcaterra thank you," I said.

"I'll let you tell him yourself. Here, take my cell phone."

"Okay," I said.

"Thank you, Doctor, for everything you've done for my mother over the years. Mom always told us that you exuded a calmness with your patients that was unmatched. Mom loved having you as her doctor."

"The feelings are mutual. Your mother is a wonderful woman. I always enjoyed talking with her. Just know that the hospice team and your family have done a great job caring for her as the end of her life approaches," said Dr. Calcaterra. "My prayers are with your family."

"Thank you," I said.

There were no more shifts. We were all in the room together now. I was happy that my sisters and I, and our children, had the chance to thank the matriarch of our family in these last days for all her unselfish work. Sacrificing for her children and helping raise her grandchildren, she traded sleep for dark circles under her eyes, forewent designer purses for diaper bags, swapped fancy restaurant dinners with Dad for homemade meals that she cooked for us, and wore old clothes so she could buy new ones for her family. Then when she became sick, she still put the lives of others before her own.

Watching my mother having difficulty breathing and experiencing choking sensations was horrible. I was determined to stay strong because of my love for the women in my family, especially the one who was about to leave us. After seven days without eating, there were no more questions and no more answers. The queen of our family was in a coma.

The last new person most people meet at the end of their life is usually a nurse, a doctor, or a chaplain. Chaplain Dorothy was that person for Mom. She met with family members often, but shared important parts of her duties with Sister Leonette, to make sure extra energy went toward Mom's spiritual needs and grief support for family members and close friends.

"Steve, blessings to you and your family, as your Mom's journey here is about to end, and about to start in a much grander place," Chaplain Dorothy said to me that morning. "Your family's faithfulness is vivid testimony of the love and care you all have for your mother. May you all take comfort from that same love."

If you study care-giving on the Internet, the marketing departments of all establishments claim to provide their clients with the best quality care in a "comfortable, home atmosphere." The marketing paints a pretty picture. Pardon me for believing that not all of them cut the mustard. It is easy for employees to ignore docile clients who never cause trouble. It is easy to keep combative patients over-medicated so they zone out and make life easy for the staff. I never saw those tricks used at Bethesda.

I know now that there was indeed no trick to it at all. What it took was planning, organization, hard work, and affection. Maybe because of the deserving way in which my mother lived her life, she deserved all the love that surrounded her. The genuine, caring conversations she had with all of us over the years were the best memories she left behind. But that big heart she had that once inspired so many others, could no longer inspire itself.

I've wondered from time to time just what my purpose on Earth entails, but of course, not all the answers have occurred to me. Mostly because of my mother, I know that I must continue to accept God in my life. We are supposed to treat others kindly and respectfully. I know that for sure, too. And I know the greatest rewards often come to us in places where we never expected anything.

Chapter 16

The shower that released itself right over Bethesda earlier in the morning raised the humidity off the charts. It was obvious that the rest of the day was going to turn out to be a scorcher. The birds in the trees were fully awake. It was the kind of day where the people working outside were anxious for their shifts to end so they could get home and shower, change into dry clothes, and enjoy their evening inside their air-conditioned houses.

It was Tuesday night, my usual night off from work. Kathy and Patti had expressed their desire to keep a close eye on things overnight. While both sisters changed into comfortable sleepwear, I went and knelt down next to my mother and whispered in her ear, "Mom, its okay to let go. There is no need for any more suffering." It was getting late, one half-hour before midnight, and Aunt Rose and I decided we were going to drive to my house for some sleep.

"Kathy and Patti, you will call Karen and me if anything happens, right?" I asked.

"Of course," said Patti and Kathy in unison.

"Okay. Aunt Rose and I will drive back early in the morning."

Twenty-five minutes later, Aunt Rose and I were standing on the front porch at my house. As soon as I unlocked the front door, I could hear my landline ringing. I rushed into the kitchen to answer it and lifted the receiver.

"Steve, Mom passed away," Patti's voice said, cracking. "We started to hear those rattling sounds in her breathing right after you and Aunt Rose drove away. At the end, she took two heavy last gasps, and that was it. Kathy and I swear we saw Mom's soul leave her body."

"Did you talk to Karen yet?" I asked.

"I hit the button on your stored number in my cell phone just seconds after Mom passed," said Patti. "I need to call Karen still."

"Okay. Aunt Rose and I are on our way back to Bethesda."

Mom's blood pressure was barely measurable when she stopped accepting food, and yet she still had lived another week. On her last day, she lay curled up on the bed and barely breathed—moving for nothing and responding to nothing, not even moving her lips when Kathy tried to put an ice chip in her mouth. She died three months short of her eighty-third birthday.

Mom died at 11:54 pm on August 20, 2014. Like the sparkles on the ocean that leave when the sun goes down, she was gone. It was exactly midnight when Aunt Rose and I headed back to the facility. The streets were dim and sleepy and looked as dead as I felt. I noticed the tickle of a tear run down my cheek.

Nurse Susan called the coroner, and we tidied up the room and said a prayer for Mom. Aunt Rose, Kathy, and I went back to my house. Karen and her husband Mike went back home to their house. Patti drove to her in-laws' house. It was a few hours before the coroner arrived at Bethesda. Because we had already gone home to sleep, and the coroner didn't talk with any family member or Bethesda employee, he took it upon himself to assume an incorrect day of death. I found out later that he recorded the date as August 21. To me, this was an insult for a woman who had paid so much close attention to details before sickness overwhelmed her abilities. I never met the coroner. Instead of making a big deal about it, I chose to look at the situation the way my mother would have, and let it go. It would mean we simply had another little story to tell.

Mom had decided to relieve a little of the pressure on me by dying on my day off, so I had no extra reason of worry about work. And she decided to die in the arms of Kathy and Patti, her two children that lived out-of-town, who had fewer chances to spend time with her than Karen and me in recent years.

"There's nothing like a good night's sleep, but last night was nothing like a good night's sleep," said Aunt Rose, still in her pajamas and night gown the next morning.

"I know. I had a restless night too, because I was

thinking about all sorts of things," I said. "So much has happened in the last year."

"We can all take comfort in the fact that your Mom died peacefully. The reality about the elderly in their final months of life, in a supervised setting, is that they nap off and on during the day, while their children run around in zombie-like circles taking care of details and going without enough rest."

"I wouldn't have wanted it any other way."

"Your mother was very grateful that her children never abandoned her during all her difficult struggles."

"Thank you," I said. "We already made all the Mass and funeral arrangements. Is there anything else you think we need to do?"

"Just remember to ask a friend or one of your brothers-in-law to help you move the furniture out of Mom's Bethesda apartment. We all need help once in a while," said Aunt Rose.

"Thanks again. Thanks for everything. Thanks, not just for your help with advice, but for your kindness. I would like to talk to my sisters about letting Bethesda keep all Mom's furniture. The sofa, the digital TV, the queen-size bed, and the maple chest are practically brand-new."

"That's a great idea," said Aunt Rose.

"I think it's a nice way to show our appreciation for the Bethesda staff," I said.

"The staff will have no problem donating the items to appreciative residents. Plenty of our elderly are scraping by on Social Security and a pittance of a pension."

Now awake, after sleeping in until late morning, Kathy walked into the kitchen.

"Bethesda is a special place, you must agree," I said.

"Whenever there is a problem, the staff takes charge and pulls together," said Kathy. "Because they understand the trick of getting the contacts and the true problem-solvers in place, they are good at minimizing the suffering of their residents."

"They are all about keeping quality of life," said Aunt Rose.

"Speaking of quality, ladies, would you like a nice late breakfast or early brunch? I'll make it," I said.

"I already have your coffee-maker going," said Aunt Rose. I'm heating up water to make some tea."

"Would you like some eggs and toast to go along with your tea?"

"Toast sounds good."

"I just want a cup of coffee," said Kathy. "I'll make it when Aunt Rose is finished making her tea."

Soon the day of the funeral arrived. Aunt Rose and Kathy sat at the kitchen table that morning for only a short time, because both were busy with laundry and ironing the clothes they wanted to wear. While the women took showers, I sat and read the Post-Dispatch. When I heard Kathy leave the bathroom and walk into the guest bedroom, I went into my own bedroom and laid my best suit over a chair. I brushed my teeth, shaved my face, and took a shower.

And so it came time for family and friends to attend the final goodbye for Audrey Hubele. When we left for the day dressed in black, the house was in order, and we could smell the aroma of summer air at the front door. As the hour approached four, from all the reaches of the city of St. Louis, cars and taxicabs formed in a long line, rolling up to park in the lot of the Kutis Funeral Parlor on Gravois Avenue. Some came in Chevrolets and Fords, some in Toyotas and Hondas. There were family members scattered around town, friends who had worked with Mom, retired friends of my father, elderly women who still lived in their own houses, old golfing buddies, members of card-playing groups and book clubs, and parishioners that knew Mom from church. All nationalities and races were represented. Inside the funeral parlor, people hugged, smiled, laughed, nodded, and told stories to my sisters and me in front of Mom's casket as they moved along in line. Touching comments and fond memories shared gave all of us hope and comfort.

Helen appeared in the doorway, and I waved at her to come toward me. As she came closer, I could see she was teetering on the cliff-edge of that unconvincing, brave stare that usually leads to tears, and seeing her kneel in front of the casket to pray and stare at my deceased mother almost sent me over the edge myself. After gazing at her friend's face for the last time, Helen turned to me with watery eyes and a vague smile. She reached for me, and I stepped over to hug her. Finally, she wept openly. I did my best to smile and appear strong.

"Because she had an uncanny ability to make a person laugh their tears away, if something was bothering me or making me sad, I always called to talk with your mother," said Helen.

"Mom told me how you and she relied on each other for support," I said. "You understood each other's worries."

"I'm really going to miss her," said Helen, her voice choking. "I guess now that your mother has passed, you'll get a look at her checkbook, and you'll find out how often she and I gambled at the casinos."

"I know you both liked to play the slot machines. Helen, did my mother ever tell you about the time we took my grandmother to the casino for a night of gambling?" I asked, hoping the story might cheer her up.

"No, I don't think so," said Helen.

"We went to the Casino Queen across the McKinley Bridge. You know where it is, right?" I asked.

"Yes, just across from downtown, on the Illinois side of the Mississippi."

"The three of us were losing money for most of the night, so we were talking about leaving," I said.

"Been there," said Helen.

"As we walked down an aisle toward the door, my grandmother suggested we make one last bet at the roulette table. 'Let's bet five dollars each on 12 and on 25, Jesus' birthday,' she said. Mom and I agreed, and we put the money down."

"Did you win anything?" asked Helen.

"The lady working in the pit spun the wheel, and we

watched as it turned and then began to slow. The little white ball bounced around for a few seconds and landed on the number 12. But the force of the wheel spinning was still strong, and the ball popped into the air and bounced around on the wheel a few more times. Finally, as the wheel came to a stop, the ball landed on the 25. We won."

"That is a great memory of your grandmother that you will have forever," said Helen.

"She died in the hospital two weeks after that night at the casino."

"Your mother never told me that story," said Helen.

"Collectively, after we cashed in all our chips at the window, the cashier paid us eleven-hundred-ninety dollars. Nine tenths of one hour is fifty-four minutes. Mom died at 11:54 p.m. It's eerie to think about," I said.

"Your grandmother and mother are together again at the roulette table in heaven," said Helen.

I hugged Helen again, and she went on her way. Then Dr. Salinas, Mom's old boss, came up and shook my hand.

"Your mother was a wonderful woman and a great nurse," he said gently. "When she worked for me, patients often asked if they could say hello to and talk to Audrey."

"Doctor, she loved working for you," I said.

"All the staff and patients loved your Mom. I'm sorry for your family's loss," he said. "Hang in there, Steve. You have my condolences."

Two more remarkable and exceptional people walked over to greet me.

"Thank you for allowing us to care for your mother. I wish you peace on your journey to live the rest of your life without her presence," said Laurel, the hospice administrator at Bethesda.

"Steve, I'm so very sorry for the loss of your dear mom. It was a pleasure for me to have cared for her. May she rest in peace," said Nurse Susan.

It was at that moment, hearing the nice words from Nurse Susan, that I realized there is a numbness that takes over the mind and body to help you get through a wake and a funeral before the hard work of adjustment begins and you try to establish a new sense of what is normal.

"Hi, you must be Audrey's son," said a thinly bearded man wringing his hands and nodding his head respectfully.

"Yes, hi, my name is Steve," I said.

"I'm Mr. Kinealy; I grew up next door to your mother and her sisters on Warren Street. Audrey was a beautiful lady."

"Thank you," I said.

"How many children did your mother have?"

"Four, I'm the oldest, and I have three younger sisters. She loved her six grandchildren and one step-grandchild."

"Spoiled them rotten, I'm sure," said Mr. Kinealy.

"I've heard about you from stories Mom and Aunt Rose told about their childhoods. I know you guys walked to the Crown Candy Malt Shop to hang out on Friday nights, and I heard you all got caught smoking cigarettes under a porch before you guys were yet teenagers."

"That's true, but I think we were all coughing more than we were smoking," said Mr. Kinealy.

"Nowadays, when you're sick and go to the doctor, the first thing they ask is if you smoke or drink," I said.

"I quit smoking thirty years ago. But when my generation was young, people were unaware of the dangers of smoking," said Mr. Kinealy. "Cigarettes were advertised everywhere."

"Mom quit smoking whenever she was pregnant, and she quit for keeps about twenty-five years ago," I said.

"Crown Candy is still in business. Do you ever go there?"

"About five years ago I took Mom and Aunt Rose there for ice cream. Afterwards, we drove four blocks to look at the house they grew up in, and an African-American mother with were her two young children, I assume, were sitting on the front porch."

"The elementary school I attended was converted into a black history museum," said Mr. Kinealy.

"Mom and I drove by her childhood home again last year, but all the houses on the old block were gone. We found out a wrecking company had raised the homes to make way for a future retail development."

"Things change," said Mr. Kinealy.

"More than we want sometimes," I said.

"What was the final cause of your mother's death?" asked Mr. Kinealy.

"She had major heart surgery five years ago. Her mitral heart valve started leaking, and she had some internal bleeding, probably in her small intestines. At her advanced age, and because she had other health issues, another major operation was out of the question."

"Was the family with your mother at the end?" asked Mr. Kinealy.

"Oh, yes. We shared in the hospice program at a wonderful place called Bethesda."

"Well, it was nice to meet you, Steve," said Mr. Kinealy. "I'm sorry about the passing of your mother."

"It was very nice to meet you. Thanks for coming. If you want to say hello to Aunt Rose, she's standing by that tan chair."

"I will. Thank you, Steve," said Mr. Kinealy.

I watched him walk over and hug Aunt Rose, and they talked for about fifteen minutes. By evening there were perhaps three-hundred people spilling in and out of the parlor. All sorts of folks came to pay their respects. Merchants from small businesses, the owner of the golf course where Mom played in earlier years, employees and ex-patients from the doctor's office where she worked, neighbors, friends, and relatives from both sides of the family came to wish her a final farewell. Even the bus driver at Bethesda, who Mom loved, and the residents living there made the effort to come to the funeral home to say goodbye to their friend.

"Steve, your mother's life is being celebrated. This is a happy scene. You can tell she was part of a much bigger family of good people," said Aunt Rose, as one of the bells from the cemetery across the street began to toll the hour.

Although everyone deals with death differently, I've learned that some things are helpful and others not so helpful when you're talking to someone who's grieving. The best thing to hear at the funeral is, "I'm sorry for your loss." Most other words that get said can be more unhelpful than helpful, even though they are voiced with good intentions. When someone says, "What can I do to help?" it puts the burden of thinking on the grieving person, who already is pressured with making decisions. Instead, cooking food and dropping it off, or offering to take the family dog for a walk, are good options to consider. Another expression you hear at funerals is, "Everything will be okay." No person who says that can guarantee the truth of that statement. Something like "I'm always here for you if you need me" sounds better. It's weird to continuously hear, "Your mother looks great," when she is lying in a casket. For me, it was hard to imagine any dead person as looking great. I liked it better when someone asked, "Did one of your sisters pick out that beautiful outfit your mother is wearing?" Before long, you can tell which people have had some training or experience dealing with death.

Choosing a funeral home or funeral service is difficult for many people. But for me, I had already worked through this process when my father died. For five generations, the Kutis family has owned and operated funeral homes in the St. Louis area to serve the community. The marketing staff at Kutis advertise "affordability and dignity" as what they want to provide to grieving families. They do indeed give quality service with compassion and respect, all at an affordable price.

Young funeral director Tom Kutis, who followed in the footsteps of four previous Kutis men with the same name, was in charge of our funeral procession to our church for Mass the next morning. He was nervous. He was new at his job and had only run processions for two other families before ours. Though his uneasiness showed, he talked to Aunt Rose, my sisters, and me with compassion and respect.

"Mr. Hubele, if you will, please, it's time for your family members to bring their cars around and line them up behind the black limousine," said Tom.

"Okay, I will tell them. Thank you, Tom," I said.

Tom's only glaring mistake occurred in the parking lot. There was another funeral going on in an adjacent parlor at the funeral home. Tom mistook one of the family members of the other funeral procession as belonging to ours and directed him to join in with the cars lining up behind the black limousine. Aunt Rose, Kathy, and I sat and watched from inside the black limousine with our driver.

"Tom is new at this," said the driver. "He is a fifth-generation Kutis."

It was messy watching Tom waving cars going in different directions, trying to correct his mistake, and directing cars to line up in their proper processions. I imagined he was perspiring profusely because the weather was already in a warm and anxious mood. Actually, Tom was entertaining us. If Mom was alive, and this was happening at someone else's funeral, she would have found it amusing, too.

Once the commotion settled, our funeral procession filed out without any more glitches. We only needed to travel about three miles alongside streets to get to our church. There was no faster route or need to use one of the interstates in town.

When we arrived, the other pallbearers—Hoff, Mike, Connor, Justin, and Cousin Dan from my Dad's side of the family—helped me carry the casket up the steps and inside the entrance of St. Simon's Church. We set the casket down on gold-plated rails that were adjusted and locked at the proper height on caster wheels, then rolled the casket down the aisle and left it in front of the altar, underneath the crucifix.

Father Erich selected a beautiful liturgy to honor our mother. "If only for a brief time you were able to walk with Audrey, you should consider your experience an honor," he said in his homily. That line was my favorite sentence of the service. I thought it was the most fitting thing you could say to honor any human being. I loved it. Father Erich added a prayer asking God for the safe delivery of Audrey to heaven.

"Catholic funeral rites are celebrations that enable the community to mourn as well as to hope. We focus on the mystery of death and the resurrection of Christ," he told us. "Death and passing on to eternal life are mysteries at the center of the Church's belief. Although American culture generally recoils from death and tries to deny it, in the face of death, the Church confidently proclaims that God has created each person for eternal life and that Jesus, the Son of God, by His death and resurrection, has broken the chains of sin and death that bound humanity."

Those words gave me food for thought. Death is a mystery to every person. If we are supposed to prepare ourselves and not jeopardize our chances for eternal life in heaven, why would anyone want to cheat, lie, steal, assault, or kill anyone?

"Therefore the celebration of the Christian funeral brings hope and consolation to the living. God tells us to turn always to Him in times of crisis," Father Erich continued.

At that moment I turned my head and looked toward the pews on the other side of the aisle. The bus driver and many of the residents and staff members from Bethesda were sitting in the middle rows. They filled five aisles of the church. I nearly broke down when I saw that they were all inside our church to honor my family. It was difficult to control my emotions, but I did, and turned my head back toward the altar.

When Mass was over, everyone filed out, pew by pew. I walked down the aisle with my left arm resting on the shoulders of my Aunt Rose and her right arm wrapped around the back of my waist. She was like a glove that fit perfectly. My sisters and their husbands and children followed and then Sister Leonette and Peggy, then other relatives from both sides of our family, then all the friends of our family that came to pay their respects. When I realized everybody was outside except for the group from Bethesda, I walked back inside the church. It was wonderful. Almost to the person, they thanked me for a lovely service, but it was lovelier for me to have this special time to cherish with them. I hugged each person individually, and as the tears rolled down our cheeks, we watched each other cry. These were the people that I loved and now considered part of my family. All the things we wished we could change, we had to tailor to a new fit. Constantly adapting is something my Bethesda friends know a lot about.

I joined Aunt Rose and Kathy and our driver in the limousine for the procession ride to the cemetery. We traveled on a bad stretch of road with numerous potholes that were recently filled with a mixture of hot tar and asphalt. After crossing over railroad tracks, we traveled along more side streets on our way to Jefferson Barracks Cemetery. We passed Dressel Elementary School.

"I went to kindergarten at that school," I said. "I doubt many children are as sad and unhappy as I was after the first couple of weeks of kindergarten."

"Why? What happened?" asked Aunt Rose.

"It was the second week of school, and I already had a crush on this little girl in my class," I said. "She had this long-sounding Russian name, maybe it was Croatian or Bosnian. None of the teachers knew how to pronounce it. All I know is that her last name sounded somewhat like 'Hilarious'. I thought her name was Debbie Hilarious."

"So tell us what happened," said Kathy.

"It was one day during the end of the second week of kindergarten. I was staring at Debbie Hilarious sitting at another table across from where I was sitting in the cafeteria, but she would never look over at me," I said.

"You poor thing," said Aunt Rose.

"Forget about feeling sorry for him, Aunt Rose. He was a little nerd back then," said Kathy.

"After the last school bell sounded on the day my stare-down with my secret crush failed, I witnessed Miss Hilarious running to her bus parked at the far end of the boarding lane, then fall down on the sidewalk. I could see she had badly scraped her knees, so I ran to the nurse's station that was next to the principal's office and asked for two Band-Aids," I said.

"Did the nurse ask who needed them?" asked Kathy.

"You know how it was back then. She probably just assumed since I asked for them, I needed them. I was in no need of emergency attention. I ran back outside and handed the two Band-Aids to Miss Hilarious, tears running down her face and blood oozing out of the scrapes on both of her knees. She said nothing, and I said nothing. I figured the silence meant that I was her hero."

"Is there some lesson to learn from this story about the first girl you chased?" asked Kathy.

"The next day I walked over to the table in the cafeteria where Miss Hilarious was sitting during lunchtime and sat next to her. I said, 'Hi, Debbie,' then asked her, 'Do your knees still hurt?' She answered, 'I'm not interested in becoming your girlfriend just because you brought me two Band-Aids. Go sit at another table,' and she used her lunchbox to push me away."

"So are you over your crush on Debbie Hilarious yet?" asked Kathy.

"You guys are cracking me up," said the driver.

"After she pushed me with her lunch box, my crush was over," I said. "I guess I learned early on that girls can act as mean as boys. I learned to appreciate kindness."

During the rest of the ride to the cemetery, we talked about Mom. "When it came to overcoming obstacles, Mom was an inspiration to others," said Kathy. "Her eyes were always full of determination. In spite of battling so many illnesses during her last ten years, she always found ways to come out on the other side of setbacks, until the last one."

"Like searchlights," I said. "Someone at the funeral parlor said that about Mom's eyes. He said they were the eyes of an archangel."

After the burial, the mourners came back to St. Simon's for a light luncheon. There's something very dear about a school and church you grew up in. I knew every nook and cranny. My sister Patti was baptized at the altar. I was confirmed at the rail and a member of the first class to complete all eight grades and graduate from the school. My family sat in a pew at St. Simon's every Sunday for God knows how long.

Aunt Rose, Kathy, and my daughters and I were now sitting at one of large round tables in the school cafeteria. Lunch consisted of ham sandwiches, roast beef sandwiches, mostaccioli, fruit salad, and vegetable h'or-deuvers. After preparing their plates in the food line, Peggy and Sister Leonette sat down and joined us at our table. We held hands, and Sister Leonette led a short prayer. When every guest was finished eating, my neighbor Mary, who volunteers at the cafeteria, brought out three large plastic containers of leftovers for me to take home. After the crowd left, Aunt Rose, Kathy, and I stayed a few more minutes to throw away used drink cups and messy paper plates and help wipe down tables.

We finally made our way out to the top front step of the church. With the clouds in the sky thickening, I looked up and then out toward the parking lot. That's when I realized our limousine driver had already left, and my truck was still at Kutis Funeral Home.

"Maybe our driver had another funeral procession to work today," I said.

"How far of a walk is it to your house, where you could get a ride from a neighbor to go get your truck?" asked Kathy.

"If I cut through the park at the end of Mueller Road, it's only about two miles," I said.

It appeared that every person who attended the lunch-eon had already left to go home. Just then I spotted a car coming around from the back parking lot. Cousin Sharon, from my Dad's side of the family, was driving the car alone. She saw me waving her down and stopped her car right in front of us.

"What's going on?" she asked.

"You're not going to believe this. Our limousine driver left us stranded here. I guess he figured we'd get a ride from a family member or friend. My truck is still at the funeral home," I said. "A young man, who is a fifth-generation Kutis, was in charge of our funeral. I guess he's still learning the ropes."

"It sounds like it. Come on, hop in my car. I'll take you guys back to the funeral home," said Sharon. "I can hear Aunt Audrey laughing at us. Maybe she planned this trick on you guys."

We climbed in, and Sharon glanced at Aunt Rose. "You never get any older-looking, Aunt Rose," she said.

"Well, thank you sweetie. I've had two knee replacements in recent years, but knock on wood, I've stayed healthy. We all complain about little things. But when we visit hospitals or go to funerals, we realize that when we have our health, we have everything."

"That's for sure," I said, nodding.

"Did all the children and grandchildren have a chance to say goodbye to Aunt Audrey before things started going downhill?" asked Sharon.

"Yes," I answered. "She talked to all of us individually, right before and during the first two or three days of hospice. I'm not sure what she said to anybody else, but I can tell you what she said to me. She told me not to cry when she was gone. She said to go outside more often when the sun is shining, smile when other people mention her name, turn away if someone purposely tries to upset me, and live my life always walking toward something, instead of running away from hard challenges."

"That's profound," said Sharon.

"Her words fit you perfectly," said Kathy. "She told me to cut down on my stress at work and to give Dave and Brad a big hug when I get back to Denver."

"Those are nice thoughts to hold onto, too," said Sharon.

Ten minutes later we were getting out of Sharon's car. The funeral lot was completely empty except for my Dodge Ram pickup.

I drove Aunt Rose and Kathy to my house, and then I went to work. The next morning dawned, and it was time to drive Aunt Rose and Kathy to the airport for their respective flights.

"I must be ready to leave in twenty minutes," yelled Aunt Rose.

"My flight leaves before yours does, and I have to be out of the house in fifteen minutes," Kathy called out from the back guest bedroom.

"Okay," I hollered back. "Then we leave in fifteen minutes."

I drove Aunt Rose and Kathy to the airport and pulled my truck into a passenger drop-off space along the curb and in front of the American Airlines terminal. Other travelers began to trickle through the doors to the terminal building waving and calling to the people that brought them.

"Thanks, Kathy, for everything. Watching you interact with the other nurses at Bethesda was amazing," I said. "Remember to do your best to cut down on any stress that comes your way."

"In the days ahead, we'll look back with pride at all the ways we came together to take care of Mom," said Kathy. "You did a great job overseeing things and building relationships with the employees at Bethesda. It helped make things go smoother at the end."

"It was good to spend time with you, Kathy," said Aunt Rose, hugging her. "Come out to San Diego and visit me sometime soon."

Kathy raised her cell phone and checked the time. "I'm not sure how much time I have to check my bags and catch my flight. I need to get along," she said. "As soon as I sit down and buckle my seat belt on the plane, grief is going to slap me in the face."

I hugged Kathy. She had never been a big crier, but her eyes watered up as she started walking away. Pulling both pieces of luggage by their extended handles, she walked inside the terminal building through the wide revolving glass doors and disappeared into the mix of other passengers.

Aunt Rose and I got back in my truck. I drove further down the lane and parked in another drop-off space, this one in front of Southwest Airlines.

"Thanks, Aunt Rose, for coming to St. Louis and helping us. You are the best. You made everything a little easier for Mom, my sisters, my daughters, and me." I hugged her with a sincerity I seldom expressed.

"When I walk through the doors, I'm not going to look back at you, otherwise I'll start crying. But please keep in touch. Call me once in a while," said Aunt Rose.

"I will. I promise. Have a safe trip back," I said, sighing like a tire losing air.

Aunt Rose walked straight inside the terminal doors, pulling her suitcase on its wheels, without looking back.

Every person handles loss in a different way and at their own pace. There is no written rule on how to grieve. If others were explicit in telling us, we would find that each experience of mourning is unique, but that the process includes phases of similar responses for most of us. In the weeks that followed my mother's death, I was constantly noticing elderly women who walked like, talked like, or looked like her. I saw an older woman at the grocery store who shuffled as she walked. I often heard older ladies talking about things that Mom talked about. The eeriest thing occurred on a Wednesday afternoon when I was driving on the interstate. When I looked over and was about to pass a car to my right, I noticed an elderly lady driving. She wore her short grey hair the same exact way as my mother. The car she drove was a green Buick, the same exact year and model that my mother drove before we took the keys away from her. When the woman turned her head to glance over at me while I passed, her face looked so much like my mother's that I gasped.

In the days that followed, I created a memorial on top of the curio cabinet in my living room. I placed a favorite picture of my mother in a frame and set it next to a favorite framed picture of my father. Behind these, I positioned a triangular glass encasement that displayed the folded American flag that was given to me by a soldier on the day my dad was buried. It commemorated his naval service, fighting in the Pacific during the Korean War. Off to the side and leaning up against the flag encasement, I stood the paper note documenting the day of the scheduled appointment at the doctor's office when my father first met my mother. I had the right to treasure these memories of my parents. Memories are one of the best legacies that exist after the death of loved ones. Instead of ignoring my memories, I was finding ways to immortalize them. My little memorial ritual did more than acknowledge the lives of my parents; it gave me private time to mourn. I sometimes wonder who it really was driving that green Buick on the interstate that day, when I gasped at the likeness of my mother. I do know there are two angels in the sky who I can now draw on for guidance. One wears a Navy baseball uniform and holds a gold baseball glove. The other is dressed in a nurse's uniform and holds a talking teddy bear.

If Allison had her way, her grandmother's tombstone would have read, "Here lies Grandma. She liked to watch game shows. She liked to make people laugh." But I decided on the inscription, "To know her was to love her; her memory lives on in our hearts." Mom always understood that good people are happier when they have opportunities to make other good people happy. She brought quiet when there was chaos, light where there was darkness, and calm to hearts when there was confusion. Her love, compassion, and courage made the world a better place. Her family and friends were lucky to have shared their lives with her and fortunate to have learned from the many lessons she taught us. In the spirit of the woman we lost, each of us was handling death in our own way, trying to bend the world a little bit in the right direction.

In her last days, our mother saw her family share memories, watched wisdoms she taught her children go into action, and put the finishing touches on her life. "How'd I end up here?" were the words Mom muttered on the first day she moved to Bethesda on Telegraph Road. Giving up the keys to her car and house was extremely difficult for her. Nurse Sylvia understood that as well as anybody, so whenever she was about to finish a procedure with Mom, she always made her laugh before leaving her apartment. "Oh boy," and "What's going on?" were two of Mom's favorite sayings.

Before I came to Bethesda, my impression of old-age homes was that they were all sad reflections of America's lack of appreciation for the elderly. We give them shelter, but we deprive them of human contact. But now I know there are places like Bethesda, where the elderly are loved, cherished, and protected. Living means that a spark is still burning inside a person, whatever their age or health status. As long as we're alive, we all crave opportunities to give and to take, to smile and to laugh, to share things with other people, and to feel the sun on their faces again.

One in six retired Americans faces the end of their life alone. If we all shared a smile or a bit of time with our elderly friends and relatives, we could brighten their days and put a sparkle into the end of their journey. We all have the same number of hours in a day. It's just a matter of choice and of setting priorities to accommodate the needs and wishes of a loved one.

Sister Leonette's visits every few days taught my family the beauty of impeding death and of God's power. From Aunt Rose, now the respected matriarch of our family, we were shown compassion and direction. From her we also learned more about our family history. It was a beautiful thing to observe everyone's commitment, just like the roles Mom wrote for us in her family Christmas plays every year.

It's sad now to think that the connection I had to my parents and the house I lived in and visited for so many years is over. But I can smile remembering all the fun I had growing up there. I can still see my mother sitting in her chair, brushing her hair. For Aunt Rose, my three sisters, my two daughters, and me, the memories will remain in our hearts, because the woman we took care of taught us how to focus on what remained in our lives, not on what was lost. And Mom herself even came to realize that it wasn't the end at Bethesda, it was only just the beginning.

One month after the funeral, my two daughters and I made a visit to Jefferson Barracks Cemetery. Amanda and Allison placed a red rose next to the headstone that marked the gravesite where their grandparents rest side-by-side.